Earth Central

Intermediate
Summer Enrichment Curriculum

Grade Levels:
4th – 6th

Length of Time:
80–90 hours

First published 2008 by Prufrock Press Inc.

Published in 2021 by Routledge
2 Park Square, Milton Park, Abingdon, Oxon OX14 4RN
605 Third Avenue, New York, NY 10017

Routledge is an imprint of the Taylor & Francis Group, an informa business

Copyright © 2008 Taylor & Francis

ISBN 13: 978-1-59363-251-9 (pbk)

Routledge
Taylor & Francis Group

NEW YORK AND LONDON

Table of Contents

Activity 1 - What's Inside the Earth?

Instructional Materials
♦ 6 large sheets of chart paper,
♦ 4 large white pieces of construction paper, and
♦ a computer with Internet access.

Background
The **scientific method** is a process developed by scientists to learn more about the world we live in. In simplest terms, the scientific method is all about asking questions, observing, making guesses, testing guesses, and trying to develop a theory.

There are four main steps in the scientific method. **Observation** is the first step. When we observe something, we use our five senses to make sense of it. During this step in the scientific method, scientists ask many questions about what they are observing. An example would be a scientist observing water beads on the outside of a glass. The question might be, "I wonder why there's water on the outside of the glass?"

The next step in the scientific method is to develop a **hypothesis**. A hypothesis is a possible explanation for the observation. There may be many hypotheses for one observation. In the example above, a hypothesis might be that the glass was leaking or got wet when water sprayed on it.

The third step in the scientific method is **prediction**. Scientists develop testable predictions about their hypotheses. Testable means the scientists will be able to create an experiment to test the hypothesis. In the example above, the scientist might develop a test in which he or she would dry the glass and fill it with water again to observe whether it would leak again.

The final step in the scientific method is to perform the **experiment**. An experiment helps prove or disprove the hypothesis. In the wet glass experiment, if a scientist discovers that water doesn't leak through the glass, he or she would choose another hypothesis. Then the scientist would again develop another testable prediction and perform an experiment to test the hypothesis.

When a scientist develops a hypothesis, makes a testable prediction, performs an experiment, and discovers that the hypothesis is correct, he or she must repeat the experiment many times. If the experiment produces the same results each time, then the hypothesis becomes a **theory**. A theory is a hypothesis that has been proven many times by many scientists.

Preparation

Write one of the following questions or statements at the top of each sheet of chart paper and place the questions around the room.

♦ What do you think is inside the Earth?
♦ What do you think happens inside the Earth?
♦ How is the Earth like other planets in our solar system, and how is it different?
♦ What do you think causes earthquakes?
♦ Complete the following phrase: The Earth is like a _____.

Gather several books about the Earth, volcanoes, rocks, earthquakes, islands, geology, and landforms (caves, sand dunes, mountains, etc.). Set up a research center where students can read the books you gathered. You could even use large sheets of crinkled black or brown chart paper and a couple of large boxes to create a cave for the research center.

A. As students enter the room, pretend to be using a shovel to dig a hole. Stop often to wipe your brow, sigh, shake your head, and then keep digging. When students inquire about what you're doing, say something like this:

"I am imagining what it would be like to dig a hole to the center of the Earth. I wonder what I would see there. I wonder how it would feel. I'm also wondering if there is a better way to get this information than digging. My back is killing me!"

B. Direct attention to the five sheets of chart paper around the room. Explain that students will form teams and rotate to each paper to answer the question or complete the phrase about our Earth. Read each question or phrase aloud before students begin.

C. Have students form five teams and assign each team to a question. Allow teams several minutes to think about the question and record predictions on the chart paper. After several minutes, ask teams to rotate clockwise to the next sheet of chart paper. Repeat until each team has visited each sheet.

D. When the rotation is complete, ask each team to bring the chart paper to a central meeting place in the room. Discuss the answers. Point out that by completing the phrase *The Earth is like* _____ students composed similes. Remind students that similes are comparisons between two objects using the words like or as.

E. Have students brainstorm a list of questions about the Earth. Record the questions on chart paper. Tell students that asking questions is the first step in the scientific method.

Note

The following Web sites were working and age-appropriate at the time of publication, but McGee-Keiser has no control over any subsequent changes. Please preview all sites before letting students view them.

F. Share the Background Information with students, then help them access the following Web site to learn more about the scientific method.

http://www.brainpop.com/science/matter/scientificmethod/index.weml

G. Have students form four teams. Assign each team a step in the scientific method (observation, hypothesis, prediction, or experiment). Provide an 11-by-17 sheet of construction paper and art supplies to each team. Instruct students to write the step and its definition on the construction paper. Then ask teams to create a visual representation of the step, such as a group of children looking at a glass with beads of water on its sides.

H. Invite teams to place the steps of the scientific method in order and share their posters.

Closure

Return to Step C and ask each team to choose a question about which to develop a hypothesis. Then ask teams to brainstorm ways to get information about the question. Have teams share their results with the class.

Extension

Challenge students to write a song to teach younger students about the scientific method. Have them use a simple tune such as "Twinkle, Twinkle, Little Star" and compose new lyrics. Have students practice and present their songs to a younger class.

Assessment

Save the chart paper that students filled out for comparison at the end of Part 1. Save copies of the songs to evaluate understanding of the scientific method.

Activity 2 - Earth Quiz

Instructional Materials
- 1 copy of **Hello, This is Planet Earth** per student ,
- 20 sheets of notebook paper per student, and
- 1 sheet of white construction or copy paper per student.

Note
All pages to be used by students or copied by the teacher will be will be shown in bold face type throughout Earth Central. To locate page numbers for any of these pages, simply check the Table of Contents located on page 2.

Preparation
Arrange the room to give the content assessment to students. You may choose to move desks around so students are not tempted to work together on the assessment.

A. Explain to students that you want to see what students know, then distribute copies of **Hello, This is Planet Earth**. Provide as much time as needed to finish the assessment.

B. Have students create a science journal. They may use crayons, markers, or map pencils to write Earth Central on a sheet of white construction paper or copy paper. Then have them draw things they believe they will learn about during the curriculum. Finally, have students select a method of binding their journals, either with staples or string. As students complete their journals, allow them to select books from the research center to read quietly.

C. Score and save the assessments until the end of Earth Central.

Answers:
1. f 2. j 3. i 4. b 5. g 6. d 7. h 8. a 9. c 10. e 11. Pacific Ocean 12. Pacific Ocean 13. The wind and Earth's rotation. 14. The gravitational pull of the moon. 15. Hurricanes are caused by large areas of low pressure over warm water in the ocean. 16. Accept all reasonable examples of the water cycle including precipitation (rain), evaporation, and condensation (clouds). 17. Climate is the prevailing weather of a region. 18. Most tornadoes in the United States occur in several states called Tornado Alley: Texas, Oklahoma, Kansas, Nebraska, and small parts of Iowa and Missouri.19. c 20. a 21. c 22. d

Closure
Lead students in a discussion about the assessment. Ask students to predict what they will learn about during Earth Central.

Hello, This Is Planet Earth

Part 1

Match the following vocabulary with its definition.

1. crust

2. plate tectonics

3. geophysicist

4. Ring of Fire

5. igneous

6. geyser

7. Pangaea

8. magma

9. gem

10. caldera

a. molten rock found inside the Earth

b. an area under the Pacific Ocean with a high amount of volcanic and seismic activity

c. a cut and polished precious stone

d. a hot spring that sends up fountains of boiling water

e. a crater caused by a huge volcanic eruption

f. the outer layer of the Earth on which we live

g. a type of rock formed when magma cools

h. a supercontinent that formed millions of years ago

i. a person who studies the movements of the Earth

j. the study of the movements of the Earth

Part 2
Answer the following questions.

11. Which is the largest ocean in the world?

12. Which is the deepest ocean?

13. What causes the currents in the ocean?

14. What causes the tides?

15. How do hurricanes form?

16. Draw a diagram of the water cycle.

17. What is the definition of **climate**?

18. Where do most tornadoes in the United States occur?

Part 3
Circle the best answers for the questions below.

19. Earth is the _____ planet in the solar system.
A. first
B. second
C. third
D. fourth

20. Earth can support life because
A. it has an atmosphere made up of oxygen and nitrogen.
B. it has trees.
C. because it rains and fills the lakes and oceans with water.
D. Both B and C

21. What year did people first walk on the moon?
A. 1967
B. 1968
C. 1969
D. 1970

22. Earth is unique because
A. it is the perfect distance from the sun to support life as we know it.
B. it has an atmosphere consisting of nitrogen and oxygen.
C. it has water.
D. All of the above.

Activity 3 - Model Earth

Instructional Materials

◆ old newspaper,
◆ (1) 12-inch round balloon per student,
◆ 4 cups of flour,
◆ glue,
◆ 4 large bowls,
◆ tempera paint (red, blue, yellow),
◆ string, and
◆ a computer with Internet access.

Background Information

By studying the way earthquake waves travel through the center of the Earth, scientists have discovered that parts of the inside of the Earth are **molten**, or liquid. The inside of the Earth is made up of four layers. The outermost layer, the **crust**, is where we live. The top of the crust is covered in dirt, plants, and water. It is six to 40 miles thick. The thinnest part of the crust is found deep in the trenches of the ocean. Under the crust is the **mantle**. The top part of the mantle and crust are known as the lithosphere. Parts of the mantle are molten. The molten areas of the lower mantle are called the athenosphere. The mantle is about 1,800 miles thick. The **core** is found at the center of the Earth. The core is divided into two parts, the solid iron **inner core** and an **outer core** made of liquid iron. The core of the Earth is always hot, around 5,432 degrees Fahrenheit. Because the inside of the Earth is so hot, layers of the Earth are able to move around. This movement will be the focus of several activities in Earth Central.

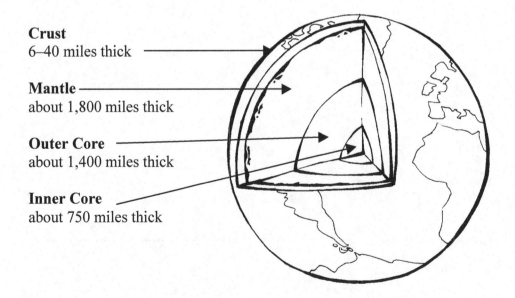

Crust
6–40 miles thick

Mantle
about 1,800 miles thick

Outer Core
about 1,400 miles thick

Inner Core
about 750 miles thick

Preparation

Find a place in your room to hang papier-mâché projects to dry. One idea is to stretch a piece of string across a corner of your room and hang the balloons from it. If you don't have a way to hang them, the balloons may be dried lying on their sides. They will need to be turned each day until dry. Drying will probably take longer this way.

Part 1

A. Instruct students to form four teams. Provide each team with an old newspaper. Have teams cover their work areas with newspaper. Instruct students to tear the rest of the newspaper into one-inch strips and place them in a pile.

B. Distribute one balloon to each student. Have students inflate and tie their balloons.

C. In a large bowl, each team should mix a paste of 1 cup of flour, 2 cups of water, and 1 handful of glue.

D. Instruct students to dip strips of newspaper in the paste, squeeze the strips through their fingers to remove excess paste, and place the strips across the balloon. They should cover the entire balloon with strips of newspaper.

E. Have students take their projects to the designated drying area. They'll need to dry for one to four days, depending on temperature, air circulation, and humidity.

F. Share the Background Information with students as they finish the first part of the project. Challenge students to draw a diagram of the Earth based on the information. Then help students visit the following Web site. As always, please preview the site before allowing students access:

http://www.brainpop.com/science/earth/earthstructure/index.weml

G. Have students record the date they completed the first part of this activity in their journals along with the following information:
♦ title of the activity,
♦ materials needed for the activity,
♦ procedure for the activity, and
♦ one thing I learned from the activity.

Part 2

H. When projects are dry, have students carefully pop the balloons inside their papier-mâché.

I. Using the diagram below, have students draw lines on their balloons and then gently bend the balloons to make it look as if one-eighth of the Earth has been removed to reveal the inner layers.

J. Review the basics of mixing paint colors with students.

red + yellow = orange
blue + yellow = green
blue + red = purple
blue + red + yellow = brown

K. Draw the following diagram on the chalkboard. Instruct students to paint the inside of the Earth first, allow it to dry, then paint the outside of the Earth green and brown (to show continents) and blue (to show oceans).

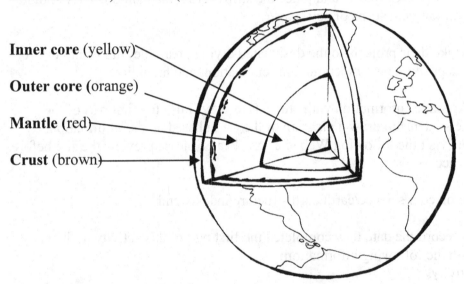

Inner core (yellow)

Outer core (orange)

Mantle (red)

Crust (brown)

L. Have students use small pieces of white paper to label the layers of the inside of the Earth. Each label should include the name and thickness of the layer.

M. Invite students to use string to hang their models from the ceiling. Students can use the sharpened end of a pencil or a single-hole punch to make holes for the string.

Closure

A. Invite students to present their models to the class.

B. Ask students to draw conclusions about the interior of the Earth. Have students write about the following questions in their journals:
♦ How do you think the molten parts of the Earth are connected with earthquakes?

♦ If the upper part of the mantle is molten, then what comparisons can you make between the crust of the Earth and a boat on the ocean?

C. Have students record the date they completed the second part of this activity in their journals along with the following information:
♦ title of the activity
♦ materials needed for the activity
♦ procedure for the activity
♦ one thing I learned from the activity

Assessment
Assess student responses in their journals.

Activity 4 – Eating the Inner Core

Instructional Materials
- 3 Nails for Breakfast kits from The Wild Goose Company,
- 3 shallow plates or dishes,
- 3 spoons,
- water,
- student journals,
- a computer with Internet access, and

Optional:
- small boxes of three other breakfast cereals that are fortified with iron.

Background Information
Our bodies need vitamins and minerals to function properly. Several years ago companies began to **fortify** breakfast cereals with vitamins and minerals to help children get the nutrition they need. One of the minerals they added is iron. Our bodies need iron to give us energy, to regulate our body processes, and to help fight illness. Iron is also an important part of our blood. By having iron in our bodies, we have something in common with the core of the Earth. The inner core is made of a solid ball of iron and the outer core is made up of molten iron and nickel.

A. Ask students to form three teams. Share the Background Information.

B. Explain that students will complete several experiments to discover iron in breakfast cereal.

C. Instruct each team to gather a Nails for Breakfast kit, a shallow plate or dish, and a spoon.

D. Have teams take out the materials in the kit. Read through the instructions for each activity to ensure students understand what is expected.

E. Distribute journals, then instruct students to write the date of the experiments and record the following information about each:
- title of experiment,
- materials used in the experiment,
- procedure (steps in the experiment), and
- what I learned from the experiment.

F. Monitor teams and answer questions. When teams have completed all three experiments, invite them to share their findings with the class.

Closure

Read the "Explanations For All" part from the experiment instructions and discuss. Then have students share why they think the title of this activity is Eating the Inner Core.

Extensions

A. Challenge students to find cereals at home that are fortified with iron. See who can bring the cereal with the most iron per serving. Take this opportunity to explain reading the nutritional information on cereal boxes. Explain that servings are different for every box and that the amount of iron fortification is probably different for every box.

B. Use cereal samples brought by students to repeat the experiments. Ask students to write and draw conclusions about breakfast cereals in their journals. Have students determine the most nutritious breakfast cereal.

C. Help students research the medical necessity of iron in our diets on the Internet. A good place to start is www.yahooligans.com. As always, please check all Web sites before allowing student access.

Assessment

Assess student journal entries for comprehension of the concepts.

Activity 5 - Digging to China

Instructional Materials
- student journals,
- 1 spoon per team,
- 1 ruler per team,
- stopwatch or watch with a second hand,
- computer with Internet access, and

Optional:
- calculators.

Background Information

Since the beginning of time, man has wondered what was at the center of the Earth. Do people live there? Do aliens live there? Is it hollow? Is it solid? Is it cold or hot? Not until the past 100 years have scientists begun to understand the **composition** of the inside of the Earth.

Books have been written and movies made about people traveling to the center of the Earth. **Jules Verne**'s *A Journey to the Center of the Earth* is perhaps the best-known book of its kind. scientists now know that the inside of the Earth is made of solid and molten areas and it would be impossible to go there. In fact, the center of the Earth is located roughly 4,000 miles below the surface. If we could drive a car at 60 miles per hour to the center of the Earth, it would take nearly three days to get there.

The deepest hole ever created in Earth's crust is over 7 miles deep. Scientists continue digging the hole to learn about the Earth's climate thousands of years ago and to study movements in the Earth's crust, including earthquakes.

Preparation

Find a place outside where students can dig holes with spoons, preferably an area with soft ground.

A. Ask students to predict the distance to the center of the Earth. Have students write the date and their predictions in their journals.

B. Share the Background Information with students. Have students calculate and share the difference between their predictions and the actual distance to the center of the Earth.

C. Tell students they will work in teams of three to calculate the amount of time it would take to dig to the center of the Earth using a spoon. Distribute spoons.

D. Draw the following chart on the chalkboard and have students copy it in their journals.

Name	Predictions	Actual	Time it Would Take

E. Have students record their names. Explain that they'll have one minute to dig a hole as deep as they can. The **depth** of each hole will be measured with a ruler.

F. Ask students to predict the depth of the hole they will dig in one minute. Have students record their predictions and the predictions of their team members in their journals.

G. Take students outside and have three students at one time dig and measure. Remind students to record their team member's actual depth dug in their journals.

H. Go back inside and help students calculate how long it would take to dig a hole to the center of the Earth using a spoon. Do a quick review of time and length measurements. Check the charts and the example problem below.

Time

60 seconds	1 minute
60 minutes	1 hour
24 hours	1 day
365 days	1 year

Measurement (Length)

12 inches	1 foot
5,280 feet	1 mile

If a student dug a hole 4 inches deep with a spoon in one minute, then:

♦ The hole would be 1 foot deep in 3 minutes. (4 x 3 = 12 inches – 1 foot)
♦ The hole would be 20 feet deep in 60 minutes. (60/3 = 20 feet)
♦ The hole would be 480 feet deep in 24 hours. (20 x 24 = 480 feet)
♦ The hole would be 175,200 feet deep in 365 days. (480 x 365 = 175,200 feet)

At this point, convert the feet calculation to miles.

175,200 feet = about 33 miles (175,200 / 5,280 = 33.18 miles)

The hole would be 33 miles deep after one year of digging.

At this point, calculate the number of years it would take to dig to the center of the Earth.

Digging at the rate of 33 miles per year, it would take about 121 years to dig to the center of the Earth with a spoon. (4000 / 33 = 121.21 years)

I. Ask students to calculate the length of time using their own measurements and record the number of years on the chart. Then have them record the time it would take their team members.

Closure
A. Discuss the likelihood of being able to dig 33 miles per year. Ask students to make a list in their journals of possible problems with digging to the center of the Earth. (The dirt and grass are only a tiny part of Earth's crust. The rest is solid rock. It would be impossible to dig to the center of the Earth using a spoon.) Ask students to include what they have learned about the makeup of the inside of the Earth in their answers.

B. Have students write two things in their journals that they learned about digging to the center of the Earth.

Extensions
A. Invite teams to research the crust, mantle, outer core, and inner core using reference materials, then ask them to write reports about each layer of the Earth.

B. Have students present their findings to the class.

Assessment
Assess student responses in their journals.

Activity 6 – Puzzles of the World

Instructional Materials
- ♦ Scientific Method posters (created in Activity 1),
- ♦ 3 copies of **Pangaea Jigsaw,**
- ♦ 3 copies of **World Map,**
- ♦ 3 copies of **News Flash!,** and
- ♦ a computer with Internet access.

Background
Alfred Wegener (1880–1930) studied to be an astronomer but decided to work in the fields of **climatology** (study of climates around the world) and **meteorology** (the study of weather). In 1915, Wegener proposed the theory of **continental drift,** which is the idea that the continents are in motion. Wegener studied maps of the world and hypothesized that all the continents had once been connected as one **supercontinent** later named **Pangaea.** Scientists disagreed with Wegener's theories at the time, but Wegener caused a **revolution** in the study of geology. Soon discoveries were made that began to prove his theory. Similar rock formations, fossils of reptiles, and fossils of ferns were found on the coasts of southwest Africa and eastern Brazil in South America. Another exciting development was the discovery of dinosaur fossils under the ice of Antarctica. Scientists believe dinosaurs were reptiles and lived in warm, wet climates, suggesting that Antarctica had once been in a place where it was warm and wet. It wasn't until 1960 that Wegener's theories were accepted by most of the science community.

Preparation
Cut apart each puzzle on the **Pangaea Jigsaw** and place them in three designated lab areas. Place copies of the **World Map** with the puzzles.

A. Direct students to three lab groups. Assign a Chief Scientist in each group. Tell students that the following evidence has been left for them to study. They are to examine the evidence (the puzzle and **World Map**) and use the scientific method to draw conclusions about the evidence. Remind students to look at the scientific method posters.

B. If students are having trouble, tell them that some scientists believe that millions of years ago the continents were once connected like a giant puzzle. Have students label the continents, then piece the puzzle together as it may have looked millions of years ago. Allow 15–20 minutes to study the evidence. Then ask the Chief Scientist in each group to get student journals. Have students write in their journals their observations about the evidence. Then ask students to formulate questions about their observations. Have students share their observations and questions with the class.

♦ Sample observations:
The pieces of the puzzle look like the continents on the world map.
The pieces of the puzzle don't exactly fit together.
The coast of South America looks like it might have been a part of Africa at one time.

♦ Sample questions:
Why were we given this puzzle and a world map?
How is the evidence we were given connected?
Is it possible that all the continents were connected a long time ago?

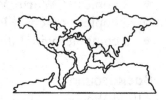

C. Ask students to write down their predictions, or hypotheses, based on the evidence they have been given. Ask students to determine what the information means. Have students share their ideas with the class. For guidance, ask students what they think caused the large landmass to separate into different continents.
♦ Sample hypothesis:
We predict that a long time ago the continents were joined together like a giant puzzle. We think the continents drifted apart because the mantle is liquid.

D. Distribute copies of **News Flash!** to lab groups. Tell students to read the new evidence. Have students write about how the evidence helps support their hypotheses. Then ask students to share what they wrote.
♦ Sample journal entry:
We already thought the puzzle we put together was like the continents we have today. The new evidence helped us see that the continents may have been connected a long time ago. The west coast of South America and east coast of Africa have fossils of plants and animals that are the same. The coal and dinosaur fossils that were found in Antarctica helps support our hypothesis because they couldn't have been there forever.

E. Invite students to draw conclusions about the evidence and form a theory. Have them write their theories in their journals.
♦ Sample theory:
Based on the evidence we were given, we have decided that the continents of South America, Africa, and Antarctica were joined a long time ago. All seven continents might have been joined at one time.

F. Share the Background Information with students, then ask the following question: How does the evidence presented today support Alfred Wegener's theory? Have students record their thoughts for the Conclusion part of the scientific method in their journals.

G. Help students visit the following Web sites. As always, please preview all sited before allowing student access.

♦ This Web site shows a list of games to help students learn geology vocabulary.
http://www.quia.com/custom/514main.html

♦ This Web site is an interactive map game that helps students identify each of the seven continents within the Pangaea.
http://kids.earth.nasa.gov/archive/pangaea/Pangaea_game.html

Closure

A. Have students discuss why it is important for us to know about Pangaea.
Possible response:

Pangaea helps explain how fossils from the same kinds of plants and animals can be found on two different continents. It also helps us understand that our continents are still in motion.

B. Tell students that Japan is about 5,200 miles from California. Researchers have determined that California moves between 1–4 inches closer to Japan each year. Ask students the following questions: (You will need to guide the thinking and help students with the multiplication. It is not important that they do the multiplication. Students should be able to tell you how the problem should be worked to get to the answer.)
♦ How many inches are in 1 foot? (12)
♦ If California moves 4 inches per year, how long would it take California to move 1 foot? (3 years)
♦ One mile equals 5,280 feet. About how long will it take for California to move 1 mile? (Rounding 5,280 to 5,000, it will take about 15,000 years – 5,000 feet x 3 years.)
♦ Japan is about 5,200 miles from California now. About how many years will it take for California to move all the way to Japan? (Rounding 5,200 to 5,000, it will take about 75 million years – 5,000 miles x 15,000 years.)

Extensions

A. Have students research Alfred Wegener's life and determine the effects of his research on the field of geology.

B. Invite students to put together a visual presentation of how Pangaea broke into seven continents. Have them make large props (draw each continent on large pieces of paper) and write a script. Then have them present their Pangaea Play to another class.

C. Invite students to go to the following Web site to learn more about Pangaea and see more video evidence that supports the Pangaea theory. As always, please preview the site before allowing student access.

http://library.thinkquest.org/17701/high/pangaea/?tqskip=1

D. Pose the following problem to students:

We know that the continents are constantly in motion. Using one of the Web sites we visited today, study the direction each continent is traveling. If millions of years passed again, can you predict where the land/continents will end up in that amount of time? Draw a picture of your predictions

Assessment
Assess students understanding of continental drift and scientific method by reading journal entries.

Pangaea Jigsaw

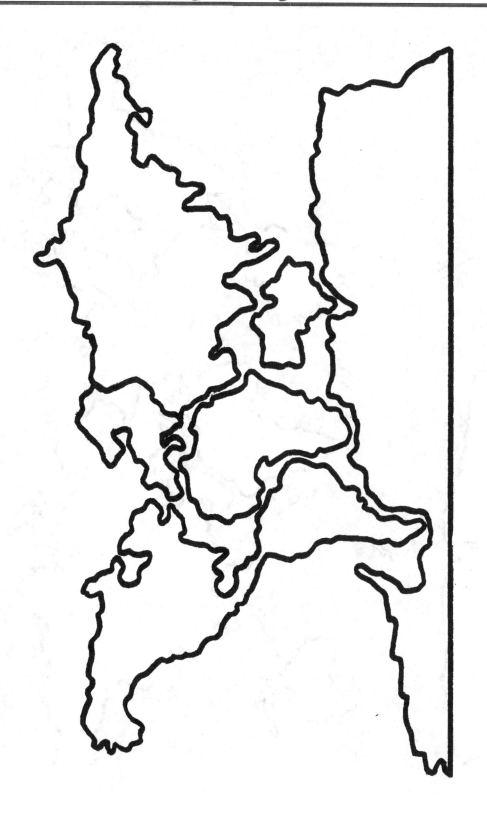

World Map

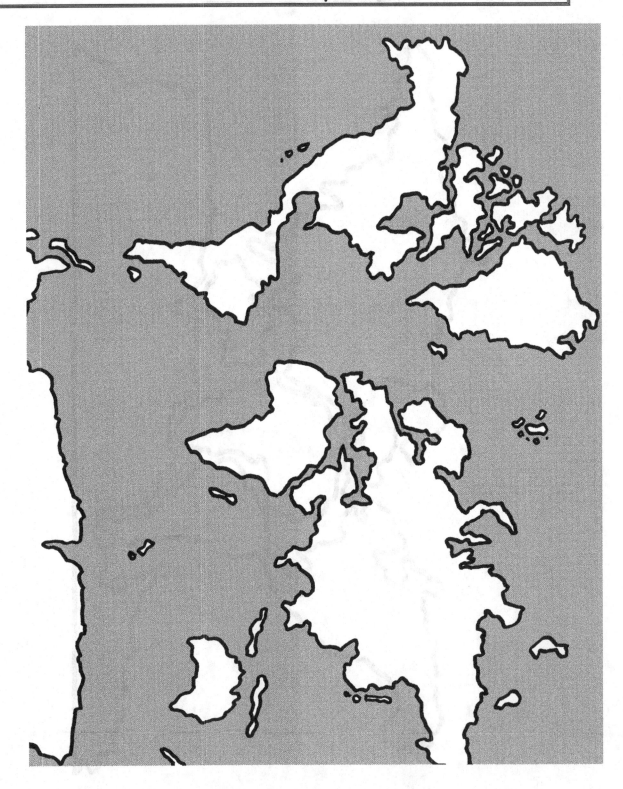

Reptiles Uncovered

By Al I. Gator

Scientists have found fossils of reptiles on the southwest coast of Africa. The amazing thing is, fossils from the same kinds of reptiles were found on the east coast of South America.

These discoveries have made scientists ask, "I wonder how the same animals could have lived on two different continents a long time ago." Scientists are puzzled by their findings.

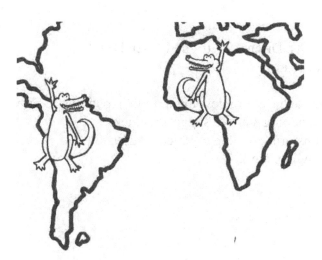

Fossilized Ferns Found

by Ima Plant

Children playing recently on the coast of Brazil discovered fossils of ferns that lived thousands of years ago. The children took the fossils home. The father of one child is a geologist, and he took the fossils to his lab for testing.

After testing, the lab discovered that the same kinds of ferns that the children found also lived off the coast of Africa. Scientists all over the world are wondering how this could happen.

Coal, Dinosaurs Discovered

By Ann Artica

Scientists in Antarctica discovered coal deep beneath the polar ice cap. They were digging in the ice to see what they could find when they hit the coal.

This may not seem strange to us, but scientist Uma Reengold explains: "We know that coal forms in warm, wet areas. Coal is made from leaves and plants that have died, rotted, and decayed on the ground. As the rotten plants sink into the ground, the ground on top of it becomes heavier and heavier. The rotten plants eventually turn into coal from the weight of the ground above."

Scientists are puzzled about this discovery. They say the coal could not have formed near the polar area because it is too cold and dry.

Another exciting discovery in Antarctica was the discovery of dinosaur fossils. Scientists believe that dinosaurs were cold-blooded reptiles that lived in warm, wet places. The discovery of fossilized dinosaur bones has scientists stumped.

Activity 7 - It's Not My Fault!

Instructional Materials
Optional:
- props for myth plays.

Background Information
A long time ago, people didn't understand many things about science. They didn't understand the sun and moon, the tides of the ocean, or great disasters such as earthquakes and volcanic eruptions. The people of long ago created **myths** to explain the things they didn't understand. A myth is a story or **legend** created to help explain something about our natural world.

In many parts of the world, earthquakes occur regularly. The people of India once believed that elephants held up the Earth with their trunks. When their trunks became tired and they lowered them, earthquakes would occur. There are many similar myths around the world.

A. Read the Background Information to students. Discuss myths and legends and ask students to retell some that they have heard or read.

B. Have students form four teams. Challenge each team to develop a myth explaining why earthquakes occur. If teams have trouble getting started, suggest a quick brainstorming session. Invite the class to brainstorm possible mythical causes of earthquakes (such as the man in the moon bowling, etc.).

Closure
Invite teams to share their earthquake myths with the class.

Extensions
A. Challenge teams to develop their myths into plays. They will need to write and memorize scripts for the characters, create a backdrop, and gather props.

B. After teams practice their myth plays, invite other classes to watch.

Assessment
Assess student understanding of myths by reading the myths they wrote.

Activity 8 – Shifting Models

Instructional Materials
- books about earthquakes,
- computer with Internet access, and
- student journals.

Background Information

Parts of the inside of the Earth are molten, and the crust of Earth is divided into several large plates. (Review the Background Information from Activity 6.) These plates are in motion as they are not attached to the mantle of Earth. Picture the crust of the Earth like 10 large boats and 20 smaller boats floating on a sea of **magma**, or molten rock. All of the boats, or plates, are touching. Some of the plates are going under one another. Some plates are going on top of others. Some plates are simply scraping by. All of this movement between the plates is happening about as fast as your fingernail grows.

When the plates of the crust move, earthquakes occur. Most violent earthquakes occur near the edges of the plates. When the plates scrape or bump together, it causes **friction**. Sometimes the plates get stuck and can't move. The friction builds up until the plates violently move apart or together. When this happens, an earthquake occurs.

Most earthquakes occur near an area around the Pacific Ocean called the Ring of Fire. The large Pacific Plate rubs against many smaller plates causing a lot of earthquake activity. Perhaps the most famous clashing of plates occurs in California. The San Andreas **Fault** is where the Pacific and North American plates come together. A fault is a fracture in the crust. California is known for many violent earthquakes. In one day, hundreds of small earthquakes, or **tremors**, occur. Many are never felt.

A. Share the Background Information, then challenge students to brainstorm ways to earthquake-proof tall buildings. Record their responses on the chalkboard. If they are having trouble, give them a hint by asking what car manufacturers do to make vehicles safer in accidents.

B. Visit the following Web sites to show examples of how architects and engineers earthquake-proof buildings. As always, preview all sites before allowing students access.

http://tlc.discovery.com/tlcpages/greatquakes/greatquakes_tech.html
http://tlc.discovery.com/tlcpages/greatquakes/greatquakes_techprotection.html
http://tlc.discovery.com/tlcpages/greatquakes/greatquakes_techapart.html
http://tlc.discovery.com/tlcpages/greatquakes/greatquakes_techplace.html
http://tlc.discovery.com/tlcpages/greatquakes/greatquakes_techbad.html
http://tlc.discovery.com/tlcpages/greatquakes/greatquakes_techfire.html

C. Have students form teams of three. Challenge each team to design a building that could withstand an earthquake with minimal damage. They should consider glass, fires, and leaking gas problems as well as structural damage. Have them draw and write about their buildings in their journals. Encourage students to use ideas from the brainstorming completed earlier as well as information from the Web sites.

Closure

Invite teams to share their building plans. Have students discuss the extra cost involved in building structures with extra safety precautions.

Extensions

A. Invite an architect to discuss the design of your school. Have him or her talk about the improvements that could make your school safer in an earthquake. Explain that few earthquakes occur in Texas.

B. Using a large world map, have students label the four major oceans: Pacific, Atlantic, Indian, and Antarctic. Remind students that the Ring of Fire encircles the Pacific Ocean. The Pacific Plate lies under the ocean. All of North America is located on the North American Plate. Have students draw conclusions as to why Texas doesn't have violent earthquakes. (Texas is not located near where two plates meet.)

Assessment

Assess the structures students designed and the reasoning behind each safety feature.

Activity 9 - Swaying Structures

Instructional Materials
♦ student journals;
♦ materials to build structures, such as dominoes, playing cards, blocks, and toilet paper rolls;
♦ several markers;
♦ several text books; and
♦ materials to absorb the shock of student-generated earthquakes, such as foam rubber, wooden blocks, and cotton.

A. Remind students there are several ways to earthquake-proof a building. Some architects construct buildings on foundations that can **absorb** the shaking of the ground. They might use things like giant springs to help a building not feel the effects of a major earthquake. Some architects design buildings that are firmly rooted to the ground and the foundation so the entire structure will remain solid during an earthquake.

B. Tell students that they will become **engineers** and **architects**, designing and building simple structures to withstand earthquakes. Provide students with materials they can use to design a building. Then have students form several teams, depending on the amount of building materials you have gathered.

C. Assign a kind of structure to each team. Each structure should be built on top of a textbook. One team should build a tall structure with some type of outside reinforcement, such as craft sticks and tape. Another team should build a short, skinny structure. Have another team design and build a structure that is large at the bottom and smaller at the top. Invite another team to design a building that is small at the bottom and large at the top. If you have more teams, encourage them to be creative in their designs.

D. Have teams turn to a blank page in their journals and record the date and title of the activity. Then have them draw a picture and label the building they designed. Have each team predict whether their building will survive a student-created earthquake.

E. Invite students to predict which building will best survive an earthquake. Have them draw the building in their journals and describe why they believe it will do well.

F. Select a team to go first. Have one team member pick up the foundation of the building (the textbook) while you slide two markers under it. Place the markers near each end of the bottom of the textbook.

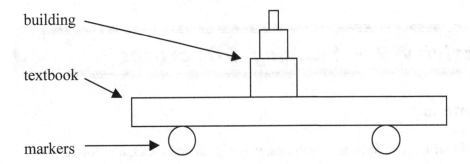

building

textbook

markers

G. To simulate an earthquake, move the textbook back and forth in two quick motions. Move the book about an inch in each direction.

Closure

A. Have students draw conclusions based on the evidence of the experiment. Ask the following questions:
- Which structure withstood the earthquake best? Why?
- Which structure held up the worst? Why?
- What are some of the problems with testing the structures in this experiment? (The earthquake test is not exact. A person trying to make the same motions with the markers and textbook is not exact.)
- What were some of the **variables**, or things that were changed, in the experiment? (building height, weight of building materials, outside reinforcement, etc.)
- If you could redesign a building to withstand the earthquake test, what materials would you use? Why?

B. Have students write in their journals about some of the things they learned about earthquake-proofing buildings from this experiment.

Extensions

A. Have the class work together to design a new building that will withstand the earthquake test. Have students discuss and then build the structure. Then ask students to draw and write about their new designs in their journals.

B. Perform the earthquake test on the newly designed structure. Have students draw conclusions about the design. Ask students the following questions.
- Was the new building design better than ones before it? Why or why not?
- Why do you think the new design was better?
- How does this experiment compare with how architects and engineers earthquake-proof buildings?

Assessment

Evaluate the Closure discussion and journal entries.

Activity 10 – Earthquakes: Attitude and Magnitude

Instructional Materials
♦ 1 copy of **A Whole Lot of Shakin' Goin' On!** for each team,
♦ computer with Internet access, and
♦ resource materials about earthquakes.

Background Information
The following Web site can be used to research some of the worst earthquakes in history. As always, please preview all Web sites before allowing students to view them. http://www.olympus.net/personal/gofamily/quake/famous.html

Preparation
Preview the Web site above to get an idea about where and when each earthquake happened. If you have limited access to computers, print out information about several of the earthquakes listed for students to use for research.

A. Have students form several teams. Provide each team a copy of **A Whole Lot of Shakin' Goin' On!**

B. Allow each team to select an earthquake to research. If you are using computers, help students navigate to the Web site and locate the earthquakes they want to research. If you printed the information from the Web site, simply hand out information to teams.

C. Write the following information on the chalkboard. Challenge students to find this information in their articles:
♦ When did the earthquake occur?
♦ What was the focus and epicenter of the earthquake?
♦ What was the magnitude of the earthquake?
♦ Describe the destruction that happened as a result of the earthquake.
♦ How much damage, in dollars, did the earthquake cause?
♦ What were the side effects of the earthquake? (fires, tsunamis, etc.)

D. Have students devise a unique way to present the information to the class. Here are some ideas for presenting the information:
♦ as a segment of a newscast, with live reports, street interviews, and a report from a scientist;
♦ in a lecture format;
♦ in writing, like a chapter in a book or a news report; or
♦ in a play format, with characters, scripts, and props.

◆ Closure

Invite students to present their information to the class.

Extensions

A. Have students videotape their presentations and share them with another class. Each team should make a "credits" card with each team member's name and role.

B. Challenge students to research other significant earthquakes and report to the class.

Assessment

Assess student presentations based on the information gathered.

A Whole Lot of Shakin' Goin' On!

An earthquake is defined as a violent shaking of the ground. The **focus** of an earthquake is the place under the Earth's surface where the shock waves from the earthquake begin. The **epicenter** is the place directly above the focus point, on the Earth's surface.

People in ancient China were the first to invent an instrument to detect earthquakes. Zhang Heng, a Chinese astronomer, devised a way to detect major earthquakes. If there was an earthquake, a metal ball fell from the mouth of a dragon and into the mouth of a frog. The metal ball indicated the direction from which the earthquake happened, and people were sent to help the victims.

Many years later, English **seismologist** and geologist John Milne invented the **seismograph**. This instrument records the waves produced by an earthquake. Since its invention, a worldwide network of seismographs has been set up. This network records more than 600,000 earthquakes, mostly tremors, every year.

The movement of the ground, or **magnitude** of an earthquake, is measured by the **Richter scale**. The Richter scale rates the destruction of earthquakes on a scale from 1 to 9. An earthquake rated as a 1 would be called a **tremor**. Only seismographs or very sensitive people would feel it. An earthquake rated a 2 would be 10 times as great as an earthquake rated a 1. It would be felt by most people. It is this way for each number on the Richter scale. So a magnitude 9 earthquake would be **catastrophic**. The highest-magnitude earthquake ever recorded in the United States registered a 9.2 on the Richter scale. The earthquake occurred in Anchorage, Alaska in 1964. Almost every building in the downtown area was destroyed. The ground in some areas cracked open and left holes 6 feet wide. The ground dropped several yards in some areas. Massive landslides covered entire neighborhoods. The death toll from this earthquake was surprisingly small because Alaska does not have a dense population.

Some people believe animals can predict when earthquakes are about to occur. Some animals become restless and begin running in circles. Others have been observed jumping before a quake. Though there is no conclusive evidence, but scientists continue to study and observe animals.

Activity 11 - Shake! Rattle! and Roll!

Instructional Materials
♦ resources about earthquakes, and
♦ student journals.

Background Information
One way we know students understand the information taught them is if they can teach the material themselves. In this activity, students will have the opportunity to create a way to teach material about earthquakes to younger students.

A. Tell students they are going to become teachers. It will be their job to write a song to teach younger students about earthquakes. Invite students to brainstorm many familiar songs, such as "Twinkle, Twinkle, Little Star." Write the songs they brainstorm on the chalkboard.

B. Have students form several teams. Each team should select a song from the chalkboard. They will then change the lyrics to teach about earthquakes. Share the following example with the class:

(to the tune of "Twinkle, Twinkle, Little Star")

Earthquake, earthquake, shake! Shake! Shake!
How I wonder how you're made.

Underneath the Earth so round,
Earthquakes start from underground.

Earthquake, earthquake, shake! Shake! Shake!
How I wonder how you're made.

C. Distribute journals so students can record their songs. Challenge students to write several stanzas to help explain the basic concepts of earthquakes.

D. When teams finish writing and practicing their songs, invite them to share their songs with the class. Be sure the class is listening carefully for information that may not be correct so the team can make changes.

E. When all teams are ready, find several younger classes to whom to teach the songs. Assign one team to each class.

Closure

Invite students to discuss the information in their songs. Ask students to evaluate their songs. Have students answer the following questions in their journals.

♦ Do you think the information you taught the younger children was appropriate for their ages?
♦ Did your team teach too much, too little, or just the right amount? How do you know?
♦ Did the younger students learn something? How do you know?

Extensions

A. Have students brainstorm other concepts that would be simpler if learned to music. An example would be multiplication facts.

B. Challenge students to write a song about one set of multiplication facts (or another subject of their choice, such as states and capitals) to share with the class.

Assessment

Assess the journal entries in the lesson and from the Closure.

Activity 12 - A Geological Loop

Instructional Materials
♦ 1 copy of **Geological Loop Game Cards**.

Preparation
Cut out the **Geological Loop Game Cards**. Here is how to play the game:
♦ Give one card to each student. If you have more cards than students, some students will get more than one card.
♦ The student with the smiley face on his or her card reads their card first. In this game, the student will read, "I have the inner core. Who has a word for molten rock?"
♦ The student having the card reading, "I have magma. Who has the deepest hole ever dug in the Earth's crust?" would read his or her card next.
♦ Play continues until the answers loop back to the first person's inner core answer.

A. Play the looping game. Time students to see how fast they can finish the loop.

B. Play a second time, but challenge students to complete the loop faster. Be sure to pick up the cards and redistribute them so each person receives a different card. Play the game several times, each time recording the time it takes to complete the loop.

Closure
Ask students to draw conclusions about the number of times the game was played and the amount of time it took to complete each loop.

Extensions
A. Have students form three teams. Challenge each team to develop a geological loop game based on what has been learned so far during Earth Central. Make copies of each game before allowing students to cut them apart.

B. Play each game that students created. If there are problems with a game, allow time for revisions.

C. Keep the games in your reference book center. Students can take turns putting the cards in the order of the loop.

Assessment
Assess student conclusions about the time it took to complete the game versus practice. If students completed the Extensions, assess their ability to create a loop game.

Geological Loop Game Cards

☐I have **inner core**. Who has a word for molten rock?	I have **magma**. Who has the deepest hole ever dug in Earth's crust?	I have **seven miles**. Who has the kind of rock in the inner core?	I have **iron**. Who has the part of Earth we live on?
I have the **crust**. Who has another word for melted?	I have **molten**. Who has a word meaning add minerals to food?	I have **fortify**. Who has the layer under the crust?	I have **mantle**. Who has the author of *Journey to the Center of the*
I have **Jules Verne**. Who has the name of the supercontinent?	I have **Pangaea**. Who has a story told to explain something in our world?	I have **myth**. Who has the word meaning rubbing together?	I have **friction**. Who has a crack in the Earth's crust?
I have **fault**. Who has a violent shaking of the ground?	I have **earthquake**. Who has a tiny earthquake?	I have **tremor**. Who has a person who designs buildings?	I have **architect**. Who has something that can be changed
I have a **variable**. Who has the place underground	I have **focus**. Who has the place on the surface that is closest to the	I have **epicenter**. Who has the inventor of the seismograph?	I have **John Milne**. Who has the country that first
I have **China**. Who has a scale by which earthquakes are measured?	I have **Richter scale**. Who has the name for the center of the		

Activity 13 – I Want to Be a Geophysicist

Instructional Materials
♦ several dictionaries, and
♦ student journals.

Background Information
Geophysics is the study of the physical characteristics of the Earth, the atmosphere and waters, and its relationship to outer space. Earth Central is an introduction to the world of a **geophysicist**. It takes a lot of hard work to become a geophysicist. At Boston College, for example, a student must take all the basic college courses such as English, history, and behavioral science. During the first two years of school, a student must take four courses in basic geology and geophysics, calculus, and physics. Later the student must take four more difficult classes of geology. They must also learn about some of the **specializations** in the field of geophysics, such as petrology (oil and gas), hydrogeology (water), and seismology, the study of Earth's movements.

A. Share the Background Information with students. Discuss the requirements to become a geophysicist.

B. Write the following words on the chalkboard:
♦ geology,
♦ geophysics,
♦ hydrogeology,
♦ seismology,
♦ technology, and
♦ paleontology.

Ask students whether they can define the words. Then remind students to think about prefixes and suffixes. A **prefix** is a group of letters that, when added to the front of a **root word**, alters the meaning of the word. A **suffix** is a group of letters added to the end of a word to add to its meaning.

C. Have students locate the prefixes and suffixes on the chalkboard. Then challenge them to brainstorm more words using those prefixes and suffixes. Have students form teams and allow each team 10 minutes to brainstorm words.

D. Invite teams to share their lists with the class. Then have students determine the meaning of each prefix and suffix from the context of their lists.

E. Provide dictionaries to each team. Have teams look up the definitions of each prefix or suffix and allow time for sharing.

Closure
Invite students to write about why it is important to understand prefixes and suffixes.

Extensions
A. Challenge teams to compose songs about what it takes to become a geophysicist. Remind them to use the information from the Background Information to help them. Have students choose familiar tunes to accompany their songs.

B. Invite students to perform their songs with the class.

Assessment
Assess the writing from the Closure activity.

Activity 14 - Earth: The Volcanic Mechanic

Instructional Materials
♦ books from the library about volcanoes, and
♦ computer with Internet access.

Background Information

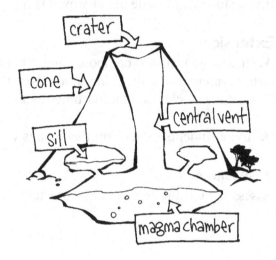

A **volcano** is a landform caused by deep cracks in the Earth's crust that allow magma to seep or explode to the surface. Volcanoes form when large pools of magma build up pressure under the Earth's crust. When the magma moves into a crack leading to the surface and enough pressure builds up, the volcano explodes.

There are many parts of a volcano. At the bottom of a volcano, usually 40–120 miles below the surface of the Earth, is the **magma chamber**. This chamber is formed when magma travels from the mantle and into the crust. When magma cannot escape through a crack in the crust, it sometimes pools and hardens, becoming a **sill**. The **central vent** of a volcano is the main tube where magma may travel through to get to the surface. The **cone** is built by numerous eruptions and is shaped like a cup near the top of the volcano. The **crater** is the opening of a volcano where the lava, rocks, ash, and steam escape.

Note
As always, please preview all Web sites before allowing students to view them.

Below are some excellent Web sites about volcanoes.

http://library.thinkquest.org/17457/english.html
http://www.fema.gov/library/volcanof.htm
http://vulcan.wr.usgs.gov/LivingWith/PlusSide/geothermal.html
http://www.k12.hi.us/~kapunaha/volcanoes_of_the_world_mai.htm
http://volcano.und.edu/vwdocs/planet_volcano/other_worlds.html

Preparation
If you don't have computers in your room, visit the Web sites mentioned above and print some of the information from each one.

A. Select one of the books you found about volcanoes to read aloud to students. Distribute journals before you begin reading and ask students to record the date, title of the book, and important vocabulary they hear.

B. Share and discuss the Background Information. Have students form five teams. Each team should select one of the following topics to research:
♦ All about volcanoes,
♦ How to be safe around volcanoes,
♦ Volcano power,
♦ Volcanoes around our world, or
♦ Volcanoes that are out of this world.

C. Once teams have chosen their topics, provide the information you printed or help them access the Web sites listed in the Background Information. As always, please preview the sites before allowing student access.

D. Challenge students to study the materials and devise a unique way to present what they've learned to the class. Here are a few suggestions:
♦ Make the presentation from the volcano's point of view.
♦ Draw pictures of the main points of the presentation and tell what was learned.
♦ Create a documentary about the topic.
♦ Make the topic a part of a news broadcast with weather and sports segments.
♦ Write and present a journal from a famous scientist studying the topic.

E. Invite students to present what they have learned to the class.

Closure

Write the topics listed above on the chalkboard. Distribute journals and have students record the following information about today's presentations:
♦ date,
♦ title of each presentation, and
♦ three things they learned by listening and watching each presentation.

Extensions

A. Obtain permission from your principal to create a Web site highlighting student research about volcanoes. You may need to enlist the help of the technology specialist.

B. Have students help plan and design the Web site. They should create a site map on paper showing the links in the site. Take digital pictures of the visuals to include with the text.

C. Add additional links and information as students complete more of Earth Central. You may decide to dedicate the entire site to the study of geophysics and have the volcano information as just one part of the site.

Assessment

Evaluate presentations and journal entries from the Closure activity.

Activity 15 - Ring of Fire

Instructional Materials
♦ copies of **World Map** from Activity 6, and
♦ 1 piece of centimeter graph paper per pair.

Background Information
The word volcano comes from **Roman** mythology. **Vulcan** was the god of fire. A volcano is a hole in the Earth's crust through which magma erupts. When magma reaches the surface, it is called **lava**. The only difference between magma and lava is where each is found.

Most volcanoes fall into three categories: extinct, dormant, and active. **Extinct** volcanoes are those that scientists believe will never be active again. **Dormant** volcanoes are perhaps the most dangerous. They appear to be extinct but can erupt without warning. **Active** volcanoes are smoking, the ground around them rumbles, and sometimes they produce lava flows.

Many volcanoes are found in an area scientists refer to as the **Ring of Fire**. The Ring of Fire basically encircles the Pacific Ocean and Pacific Plate. The Pacific Plate is bumping against and going under several of the plates around it. When this happens, magma can escape to the surface and volcanoes occur. Though California would be considered a part of the Ring of Fire, it doesn't have any volcanoes because there aren't any magma pools under it. Farther north in Washington state and Alaska, there are many volcanoes. Across the Pacific Ocean to Japan, there are 77 volcanoes. There are more than 900 volcanoes located just in the top 10 countries with volcanoes in the world.

The tallest mountain in the world is also a volcano. **Mauna Kea** in Hawaii is just over 33,000 feet tall from its base at the bottom of the ocean to its peak. Many people mistake Mount Everest as the tallest mountain, but technically this is incorrect.

A. Have students go back through the Background Information from Activities 13–15 and record all of the bolded vocabulary words on the chalkboard.

B. Have the class work together to define each word.

C. Challenge students to work as partners to create crossword puzzles using the vocabulary words as clues. For younger students, a word find might be more appropriate. Provide graph paper for the puzzles. Remind students to blacken squares that aren't used.

D. Make copies of completed crossword puzzles and the answer keys, then allow time for students to trade and work one another's puzzles.

Closure

A. Ask students the following question: Now that scientists know about and understand what causes the Ring of Fire, why do you think so many people choose to live there despite the danger?

B. Continue the discussion by asking the following question: Why do you think people live in the following places? Texas (where tornadoes often occur), California (where earthquakes often occur), and Mississippi (where flooding often occurs)

Extensions

A. Challenge students to research and map the Ring of Fire using the **World Map**. Have students write an essay explaining why the Ring of Fire is located in this area.

B. Have students make copies of their originals and bind them into a puzzle book to place in the library.

C. Have students research the ramifications of a volcanic blast, such as earthquakes, **tsunamis** (giant tidal waves), and mud flows. Invite students to present their findings. Have students discuss whether the actual eruption or the aftermath would be more deadly.

D. Have students research some of the tallest mountains in the world. Challenge students to make a bar graph comparing the tallest mountains to Mauna Kea. Then have students determine the difference in height of each mountain to Mauna Kea.

Assessment

Assess the crossword puzzles and word finds created by students.

Activity 16 – Islands From Disaster

Instructional Materials
- *The Magic School Bus Blows Its Top* book, by Gail Herman,
- *The Magic School Bus Inside the Earth* book, by Joanna Cole,
- student journals, and
- a computer with Internet access.

Background Information
The Hawaiian **island chain** has been formed over thousands of years by cracks in the Earth's crust. Some of the islands are extinct while others are very active. As the plate that Hawaii is a part of moves, volcanoes erupt and the islands grow. As an island moves away from the central vent where magma flows up through the Earth's crust, the volcano (island) becomes extinct and another island begins to form. Many islands got their start as volcanoes under the ocean.

A. Read *The Magic School Bus Blows Its Top* aloud. Ask students the following questions as you read:
- What important fact did we learn on the third page? (The Earth is always changing.)
- Where did Ms. Frizzle take the class to find the new island? (the ocean)
- What did the class discover at the bottom of the ocean? (a huge underwater mountain)
- What did the kids discover at the bottom of the canyon? (chimneys, earthquakes, magma, and a volcano)
- Where was the school bus in the volcano? (the magma chamber)
- How will the new island form? (When the volcano explodes, the lava will cool and harden on top of the underwater mountain until the mountain sticks out of the water and becomes an island.)

B. Have students form four teams. Challenge each team to record in their journals things that couldn't have really happened in the book. Have students share their lists.

C. Read aloud *The Magic School Bus Inside the Earth*. Ask the following questions as you read:
- Notice Ms. Frizzle's clothes in each picture. What clues do you have as to what the book will be about? (She starts out in a pterodactyl dress, then has a dress with screws, a dress with shovels, and finally a suit with rocks on it.)
- What are rocks made of? (minerals)
- How did Ms. Frizzle find a way to take the kids looking for rocks? (The bus dug a hole in the schoolyard so the kids could find rocks.)
- What is soil made of? (ground-up rock, clay, dead leaves, sticks, and pebbles)
- What did the kids learn about rock? (Even though there is soil and grass on top of the crust, there is always rock underneath it.)

- What are **sedimentary** rocks? (rocks that are formed when layers of sand and dust harden to become rocks)
- What are **metamorphic** rocks? (rocks that have been exposed to heat and pressure that were changed from one kind of rock to another)
- What kind of rock does limestone change into when it is exposed to heat and pressure? (marble)
- What are **igneous** rocks? (rocks formed when lava cools)
- What are the three basic shapes of volcanoes? (cinder cones, composites, and shields)

D. Challenge each team again to record things in their journals that couldn't have really happened in the second book. Have students share their lists.

E. Draw a Venn diagram on the chalkboard. On one side of the Venn diagram write "The Magic School Bus Blows Its Top." On the other side of the diagram write "The Magic School Bus Inside the Earth." Where the two circles intersect, write "Same."

F. Enlist the help of students to compare the two books. Things that were the same about the two books should be listed in the area where the two circles intersect.

Closure
Have students write a paragraph telling what they learned about volcanoes by reading *The Magic School Bus Blows Its Top*. Also have them write a paragraph telling what they learned about the inside of the Earth by reading *The Magic School Bus Inside the Earth*.

Extensions
A. Open *The Magic School Bus Inside the Earth* to a page with writing done by a student in Ms. Frizzle's class. Open the other book to any page. Ask students to examine both books and find a major difference. (*The Magic School Bus Inside the Earth* has essays and reports by Ms. Frizzle's students. The other book doesn't have any essays or reports.)

B. Reread *The Magic School Bus Blows Its Top*, having students listen for places where they could write a short report to accompany the book. Have students record ideas in their journals as you read.

C. Invite students to share their ideas with the class. Have each student choose one report or essay to write. Be sure everyone chooses a different topic. Students may choose to work in pairs to complete this project.

D. Allow students to use the books you've collected about volcanoes and help them use the Internet to conduct their research.

E. Invite students to share their reports with the class. Display *The Magic School Bus Blows Its Top* and the reports on a table for other classes to read.

F. Have students write book reviews for each of the books and add them to the Web site they began creating in Activity 14. If students didn't create a Web site, have them post their book reviews on a bulletin board outside the classroom for others to read.

Assessment
Evaluate student journal entries from the Closure activity.

Activity 17 – Make a Volcano

Instructional Materials
♦ student journals.

♦ **Ingredients for Edible Volcano**
(1) ½ gallon of rocky road ice cream,
1 ice cream scooper,
1 jar of marshmallow cream,
1 bunch mint leaves,
1 jar cherry ice cream topping,
1 cookie sheet pan with 1 inch sides, and
copies of **Edible Volcano.**

♦ **Ingredients for Papier-Mâché Volcano**
1 newspaper,
masking tape,
1 cup of flour,
1 large bowl,
glue,
1 large piece of cardboard,
aluminum foil, and
copies of **Papier- Mâché Volcano.**

1 small medicine cup,
baking soda,
vinegar, and
red food coloring.

♦ **Ingredients for Plaster of Paris Volcano:**
plaster of Paris,
water,
bowl,
stirring stick,
facial tissues,
cone shaped disposable drinking cups, and
eruption ingredients listed earlier.

♦ **Ingredients for Sandbox Volcano:**
sandbox with sand,
water,
eruption ingredients listed earlier, and
copies of **Sandbox Volcano.**

Eruption Ingredients:

Preparation

Before this activity, present the different kinds of volcanoes to students to enlist their help providing **ingredients**. Determine which type of volcano each student would like to make and group them accordingly. Make copies of **Supply Request** and have students divide the needed supplies among themselves. Double check each team to be sure all supplies are being covered.

Find parent volunteers to help each team complete its project. Borrow trays or plates and spoons from the cafeteria to serve the edible volcano quickly after eruption.

Familiarize yourself with the instructions for using plaster of Paris before starting the project.

A. After teams bring supplies, check to see that each team has everything it needs.

B. Assign a parent-volunteer to each team before beginning. Instruct teams to read all instructions carefully before they start.

C. Walk around to be sure all teams are on task. Take pictures as teams work, as they finish, and as volcanoes begin erupting.

D. Serve the edible volcano to your class. Don't forget your volunteers!

Closure
Have students write in their journals the steps to making the volcano they created.

Extensions
Add the pictures of the volcanoes to the Web site created earlier. If you did not create a Web site, have students decorate a bulletin board outside the classroom with pictures and descriptions of their volcanoes.

Assessment
Assess the success of the volcano construction and writing in student journals.

Supply Request

Dear Parents,

We are studying volcanoes in our Earth Central program. In the next few days we will be making volcanoes. You can help by sending the following item to school:

_____

Please send the item by _____

Thanks!

Dear Parents,

We are studying volcanoes in our Earth Central program. In the next few days we will be making volcanoes. You can help by sending the following item to school:

_____

Please send the item by _____

Thanks!

Dear Parents,

We are studying volcanoes in our Earth Central program. In the next few days we will be making volcanoes. You can help by sending the following item to school:

_____

Please send the item by _____

Thanks!

Edible Volcano

Ingredients:
♦ ½ gallon of rocky road ice cream,
♦ 1 ice cream scooper,
♦ 1 jar of marshmallow cream,
♦ 1 bunch of mint leaves,
♦ 1 jar of cherry ice cream topping, and
♦ 1 cookie sheet pan with 1 inch sides.

Instructions
1. Wash your hands with soap and water.

2. Open the ice cream and begin scooping it onto the cookie sheet. Build your volcano base first, then continue building up the sides to a peak. Work quickly, as the volcano will begin to melt.

3. Use your hands to shape the ice cream into a volcano shape.

4. Pour marshmallow topping on the volcano to simulate snow.

5. Pour cherry topping on the volcano to simulate a lava flow.

6. Tear off sprigs of mint to decorate the volcano with "trees."

7. Take a picture of your edible volcano.

8. Enjoy!

Papier-Mâché Volcano

Instructional Materials

♦ 1 newspaper,
♦ masking tape,
♦ 1 cup of flour,
♦ 1 large bowl,
♦ glue,
♦ 1 large piece of cardboard,
♦ aluminum foil,
♦ 1 small medicine cup,
♦ 1 teaspoon of baking soda,
♦ vinegar, and
♦ red food coloring.

Instructions

1. Tear half of the newspaper into 1-inch strips. Make large paper balls out of the remaining newspaper. Cover the cardboard with aluminum foil. Use masking tape to secure the foil to the cardboard. Use masking tape to secure the paper balls to the cardboard. Shape the paper balls into a volcano shape. Use tape to help shape the volcano. Make an indention in the top of the volcano for the medicine cup to rest.

2. In the large bowl, mix flour, glue, and water into a mixture about the thickness of runny pancake batter.

3. Dip strips of newspaper into the flour and glue mixture. Remove excess mixture by running the strip of newspaper between your fingers. Cover the volcano with strips of paper dipped in the mixture.

4. Allow the volcano to dry for two or three days. When it's dry, you may choose to paint it with brown tempera paint. You can also gather twigs and grass to make it look more authentic.

5. To make the volcano erupt, first place 1 teaspoon of baking soda in the medicine cup. Then drop in 3-4 drops of red food coloring. Place the medicine cup in the top of the volcano. Pour vinegar into the medicine cup and watch the volcano erupt!

Plaster of Paris Volcano

Instructional Materials
- plaster of Paris,
- water,
- bowl,
- stirring stick,
- facial tissues,
- cone-shaped disposable drinking cups,
- 1 small medicine cup,
- 1 teaspoon of baking soda,
- vinegar, and
- red food coloring.

Note
This activity should be completed only with adult supervision. Students should not handle the plaster of Paris mixture.

Instructions
1. Read the instructions for handling plaster of Paris carefully before beginning.

2. Before mixing the plaster, provide each student with a cone-shaped disposable drinking cup and a facial tissue. Have students stuff the facial tissue into the bottom of the cup tightly. This will prevent the plaster mixture from filling the end of the cup and will leave an indention in the top of the "volcano" for the eruption ingredients.

3. Mix the plaster according to instructions. Quickly fill each student's cup with the mixture. Place the cups in a safe area to dry.

4. When the mixture has hardened, tear the cup off the plaster, revealing the volcano. Remove the facial tissues from the volcanoes.

5. To make the volcano erupt, first place 1 teaspoon of baking soda in the top of the volcano. Then drop in 3–4 drops of red food coloring. Pour vinegar onto the baking soda and watch the volcano erupt!

Sandbox Volcano

Instructional Materials
♦ sandbox with sand,
♦ water,
♦ 1 small medicine cup,
♦ 1 teaspoon of baking soda,
♦ vinegar, and
♦ red food coloring.

Instructions
1. Wet the sand so you can build a large volcano in the sandbox.

2. Build a large volcano with a crater for the medicine cup.

3. To make the volcano erupt, first place 1 teaspoon of baking soda in the medicine cup. Then drop in 3-4 drops of red food coloring. Place the medicine cup in the top of the volcano. Pour vinegar into the medicine cup and watch the volcano erupt!

4. For a larger eruption, use a 20-ounce empty soda bottle with 3 tablespoons of baking soda, several drops of food coloring, and 2 cups of vinegar. Simply build the volcano around the 20-ounce bottle.

Activity 18 - Famous Volcanoes

Instructional Materials
- computer with Internet access,
- books about volcanoes,
- copies of **World Map** from Activity 6, and
- student journals.

Background Information
Throughout history, volcano eruptions have caused much damage. From **tsunamis** wiping out entire islands to **mud flows** destroying entire cities, volcanic eruptions can be devastating. Ancient writing in books and pictures drawn on walls depict volcanic eruptions and the damage they caused hundreds, even thousands of years ago.

Preparation
Go to www.yahooligans.com and look up information on notable volcanoes by typing the following names into the search area:
- Krakatau,
- Mount St. Helens,
- Vesuvius,
- Etna,
- Mauna Kea, and
- Pinatubo.

Each volcano has numerous Web sites. Select and bookmark one site per volcano for later use. If you have limited access to computers, print information about each volcano for use in the classroom.

A. Tell students they will research some prominent volcanoes during this activity. Ask students to brainstorm volcanoes. List them on the chalkboard.

B. Have students form six teams. Assign each one of the volcanoes listed above. Have teams research and write reports about their volcanoes. Teams should include the following information in their reports:
- location of volcano,
- date or dates of significant eruptions,
- why the volcano is famous,
- the damage caused by the volcano,
- the cities near the volcano that could be affected by another eruption, and
- a map showing where the volcano is located (Use copies of **World Map**).

C. Have teams trade completed reports for peer editing.

D. After revisions, invite teams to share their reports with the class.

Closure
Have students answer the following question in their journals.
♦ Why do you think people travel to an area near a volcano that has recently erupted?
♦ Would you want to go to see a volcano that has recently erupted? Why or why not?

Extension
Have students add the information from their reports to the Web site created earlier. If a Web site was not created, have students create a bulletin board showcasing the different famous volcanoes.

Assessment
Assess student reports and journal entries from the Closure activity.

Activity 19 – Oh, Great Volcano!

Instructional Materials
♦ books about volcanoes, and
♦ student journals.

Background Information
According to Hawaiian myth, there was once a beautiful **goddess** named **Pele**. She was known as the goddess of the Earth and fire. She was a very kind goddess unless she was crossed; then her punishment was severe.

She fell in love with the god of water, **Kamapuaa**. They were eventually married, but their marriage was anything but happy. Pele was very jealous and it wasn't long before Kamapuaa displeased her. She became angry and violent. Because she was the goddess of fire, she spat him out of her crater of fire. Then she sent streams of lava after him. The lava chased him all the way back to the ocean, where he remains.

A. Read the Background Information to students. Ask students to guess why the story was written.

B. Have students form several teams. Challenge them to write a myth about a volcano they have read about or a totally new volcano that popped up in the schoolyard.

C. Have students illustrate and present their myths to the class.

Closure
Have students summarize a favorite volcano myth they heard during this activity.

Extensions
Challenge students to develop their myths into plays, with props, songs, and scripts. Be sure that each person on a team has a speaking part. Get permission for your students to present their plays to other classes. After practicing, have students present their plays to the class. Take pictures to post on your Web site if you are developing one.

Assessment
Assess student-generated myths and the summaries in their journals.

Activity 20 – Volcano Olympics

Instructional Materials
♦ student journals,
♦ copies of **The Volcano Olympians** for each team, and
Optional:
♦ calculators.

Background Information
The speed of lava flows from volcanoes varies greatly. Factors affecting the flow include temperature, slope of the flow, and the type of lava. The fastest flowing lava flows in tubes underground or in channels. Here the lava is **insulated**. The hotter the lava remains outside the volcano, the faster it will travel. Lava in tubes or channels can flow in excess of 35 miles per hour. Lava in the open with no slope can flow as slow as ½ mile per hour.

A. Have students form teams of three and distribute copies of **The Volcano Olympians**.

B. Have teams work together to read the article and solve the problems on the page.

Closure
Invite students to share their answers with the class.

Answers:
1. ½ hour; 2. a; 3. about 2 ½ hours; 4. 45 hours.

Extensions
A. In their journals, have students draw conclusions about why volcanoes did better in sports that used tracks or tubes through which to flow. (Possible conclusions: Lava flows faster in tubes because it stays hotter.)

B. Share and discuss the Background Information.

Assessment
Some students may not know how to multiply and divide to solve the problems. Check to see that the solution process was correct (i.e., students selected the correct operation to solve the problems).

The Volcano Olympians

Volcanoes Participate in the Olympics

By Icene Etall

The International Olympic Committee overwhelmingly voted to allow volcano participants in this year's winter Olympics. Even though volcanoes got the go ahead, only volcanoes from two countries decided to participate: the American volcano, Mauna Loa and the Italian volcano, Mt. Etna.

Men's Downhill Skiing
Gold: Dante Slides of Austria
Silver: Jaques Trudeaux of France
Bronze: Mauna Loa of the United States

Men's Cross Country Skiing
Gold: Bill Swenson of Germany
Silver: Enrique Brit of France
Bronze: Mt. Etna of Italy

In the events listed above, you can see that the volcano Olympians dominated the sports that use confined tracks or tubes. People dominated the sports where they were in control of where they were going.

The average human speed on downhill skiing was about 85 miles per hour. Volcano speed on the same slope was about 6 miles per hour. Human speeds on cross country skiing ranged from 15 to 20 miles per hour. Volcano speeds dropped to around 1 mile per hour.

Volcanoes participate in the winter Olympics by erupting. The lava flows created by the volcanoes race against other participants. Some countries refuse to participate with the volcanoes, saying that volcanic lava is a danger to their athletes. Most countries agree that skiing or sledding around lava adds another element of excitement.

Men's Bobsledding
Gold: Mt. Etna of Italy
Silver: Mauna Loa of the United States
Bronze: Team of Jamaica

Men's Luge
Gold: Mauna Loa of the United States
Silver: Mt. Etna of Italy
Bronze: Ingrid Herpoff of Germany
to 20 miles per hour. Volcano speeds dropped to around 1 mile per hour.

Because the volcanoes were allowed to go first, people had trouble beating them in the bobsledding and luge categories. The volcanoes averaged speeds around 35 miles per hour in both sports. Normally human bobsledding participants reach speeds of 90 miles per hour and human luge participants reach 75 miles per hour. The lava slowed participants. Many could not finish the race because the heat melted their equipment. The Olympic Committee is now considering having the volcanoes participate only in the X-Games after this year.

Instructions

Read the unusual article on the previous page. Use the information in the article to answer the following questions.

1. The average speed of humans skiing on a downhill slope is 85 miles per hour. If the course was 3 miles long, about how long would it take for a volcano to finish erupting down the course?

2. In the question above, about how long do you think it would take a human to finish the course?
A. about 5 minutes
B. about 20 minutes
C. about 25 minutes
D. about 30 minutes

3. The average speed of humans in cross country skiing is about 17 miles per hour. If the course was 45 miles long, about how long would it take a human to complete it?

4. The average speed of the lava flow in cross-country skiing is about 1 mile per hour. How long would it take for the lava flow to reach the finish line in a 45-mile course?

Now create more silly lava Olympic questions of your own.

Activity 21 – Chocolate Lava

Instructional Materials
♦ 1 bottle of thick chocolate syrup (refrigerated),
♦ 1 bottle of lite (runny) maple syrup (refrigerated),
♦ 1 cookie sheet,
♦ 1 empty wrapping paper roll (cut in half lengthwise to form two long troughs),
♦ 1 ruler,
♦ 1 clock,
♦ student journals, and
♦ a computer with Internet access.

Background Information
Each active or dormant volcano contains magma that is different. The difference in lava is caused from the type of rocks that were melted to create it. Some lava is more **viscous**, sticky and thick. This lava tends to flow more slowly.

Some factors affecting the flow of lava include temperature, **slope** of the flow, and the type of lava. The fastest flowing lava flows in tubes underground or in channels. Here the lava is **insulated**. The hotter the lava remains outside the volcano, the faster it will travel.

Preparation
Place the chocolate and maple syrup in the refrigerator several hours before the activity. If you don't have a microwave nearby for heating the syrups, borrow a large bucket of very hot water from the cafeteria. When you're ready to heat the syrups, submerge the bottles for 5–10 minutes.

Cut the wrapping paper tube in half lengthwise so that you have two long troughs.

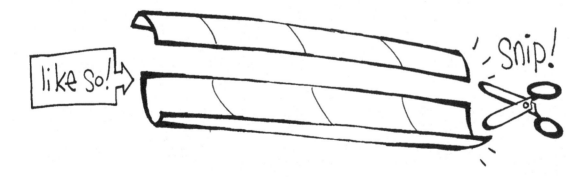

A. Share the Background Information and ask students to discuss how the last activity relates to the Background Information.

B. Distribute student journals. Turn to **Lava Experiments** and ask for volunteers to help you complete each part of the experiment.

C. Be sure students record information from the experiment in their journals.

Closure
Have students discuss the experiments, then write to the following prompts in their journals:
♦   How does this experiment demonstrate the factors affecting the ways lava flows?
♦   If you lived near a volcano, what would you want the geography (hills, rivers, valleys) to look like? Why? Draw a picture to go along with your answer.

Extensions
A. Invite students to use the computer to research how lava flows, using www.yahooligans.com. As always, please preview any sites before allowing students to view them.

B. Have students compile information about lava flows into a report to be posted on the Web site, if applicable. Be sure to include digital pictures of students completing the experiments.

Assessment
Assess student journal entries in the Closure activity.

Lava Experiments

Instructional Materials
- 1 bottle of thick chocolate syrup (refrigerated),
- 1 bottle of lite (runny) maple syrup (refrigerated),
- 1 cookie sheet,
- 1 empty wrapping paper roll (cut in half to form 2 long troughs),
- 1 ruler,
- 1 clock, and
- student journals.

Part 1—Experiments with Cold Syrups
Experiment 1—No Slope
1. Squeeze out a silver dollar sized portion of chocolate and maple syrups on opposite ends of the cookie sheet. Quickly measure the **diameter**, distance across, of each portion and record the results in your journals.

2. Allow the syrups to sit for five minutes. Measure and record the diameters again.

3. Answer the following questions in your journals:
- Which syrup spread more? Why?
- How does this experiment relate to lava flow?

Experiment 2—Slope Added
1. Squeeze out a silver dollar sized portion of chocolate and maple syrups on the same end of the cookie sheet. Be sure the syrups are in line with one another.

2. Place 2–3 textbooks under the end of the cookie sheet where the syrups are located.

3. Allow the syrups to run for 3 minutes. Measure and record in your journals the distance each traveled.

4. Answer the following questions in your journals:
- Which syrup ran more? Why?
- How does this experiment relate to lava flow?

Experiment 3—Tubes with Slopes
1. Place the ends of each tube on the stack of textbooks from the last experiment.

2. Squeeze a silver dollar sized portion of chocolate and maple syrup into each sloped tube.

3. Allow the syrups to run for 3 minutes. Measure and record in your journals the distance each traveled.

4. Answer the following questions in your journals:
- ◆ Which syrup ran more? Why?
- ◆ Was there a difference in the distance the lava traveled in the tube compared to the cookie sheet? If so, why?
- ◆ How does this experiment relate to lava flow in tubes?

Note:
At this time, the syrups should be heated for the next set of experiments.

Part 2—Experiments with Hot Syrups
Experiment 1—No Slope
1. Squeeze out a silver dollar sized portion of heated chocolate and maple syrups on opposite ends of the cookie sheet. Quickly measure the **diameter**, distance across, of each portion and record the results in your journals.

2. Allow the heated syrups to sit and cool for five minutes. Measure and record the diameters again.

3. Answer the following questions in your journals.
- ◆ Did the hot or cold syrups spread more? Why?
- ◆ Which of the two syrups spread the most? Why?
- ◆ How does viscosity (stickiness) affect the flow of the syrups?

Experiment 2—Slope Added
1. Squeeze out a silver dollar sized portion of heated chocolate and maple syrups on the same end of the cookie sheet. Be sure the syrups are in line with one another.

2. Place 2–3 textbooks under the end of the cookie sheet where the syrups are located.

3. Allow the syrups to run for 1 minute. Measure and record in your journals the distance each traveled.

4. Answer the following questions in your journals:
- ◆ How does heating the syrup affect the time it takes for it to run?
- ◆ Which syrup ran more? Why?
- ◆ How does this experiment relate to lava flow on a slope?

Experiment 3—Tubes with Slopes
1. Place the ends of each tube on the stack of textbooks from the last experiment.

2. Squeeze a silver dollar sized portion of heated chocolate and maple syrup into each sloped tube.

3. Allow the syrups to run for 1 minute. Measure and record the distance each traveled in your journals.

4. Answer the following questions in your journals:
♦ Which syrup ran more? Why?
♦ Was there a difference in the distance the heated lava traveled in the tube compared to the cookie sheet? If so, why?
♦ How does this experiment relate to lava flow in tubes?

Part 3—Drawing Conclusions
Answer the following questions in your journal.
♦ What does this experiment tell you about the way lava flows?
♦ If chocolate and maple syrup are like lava, how does it flow the fastest?
♦ What do you think causes lava to flow more slowly?

Activity 22 - Deep-Sea Relationships

Instructional Materials

♦ 3 copies of **Discoveries,**
♦ *Fountains of Life The Story of Deep-Sea Vents* book, by Elizabeth Tayntnor Gowell,
♦ student journals, and
♦ s computer with Internet access.

Background Information

For thousands of years people wondered what was at the bottom of the ocean. Nautical fantasies describe colonies of mermaids, Atlantis, and giant sea monsters capable of destroying a sea vessel with one swipe of a tail or tentacle.

The human fascination with life under the sea is timeless. As early as 1690 people have tried to devise ways to get to the bottom of the ocean. The problems associated with traveling so deep are lack of oxygen and extreme water pressure. It wasn't until the 1960s that people finally learned what was at the bottom of the ocean.

In 1977 a group of scientists was studying temperatures deep on the ocean floor. When the temperature of the nearly freezing water increased slightly, the scientists were baffled.

Eventually they used a **submersible**, a vehicle designed to travel to great depths in the ocean, to investigate. What they discovered was giant cracks in the Earth's crust that allowed hot steam and water to escape. The steam and boiling hot water is what made the water temperature rise. When the scientists finally reached the place where the water temperature was warmer, they were surprised to discover a colony of unusual sea creatures living near what they called **deep-sea vents**. There were giant tubeworms, giant clams, and even crabs. These sea creatures would not be able to survive without the warmth provided by the deep-sea vents.

A. Have students form three teams. Provide each team with a copy of **Discoveries**. Have students read the articles and then use the scientific method posters to hypothesize, predict, and draw conclusions based on the observations in the articles. Have students record the following information in their journals:
♦ hypothesis about articles,
♦ prediction about articles, and
♦ conclusions about articles.

B. Have students share their hypotheses, predictions, and the conclusions they drew with the class. Discuss each set of conclusions and the likelihood of each before moving on.

C. Read aloud Chapter 3 of *Fountains of Life The Story of Deep-Sea Vents* aloud and discuss. Have students compare their hypotheses, predictions, and conclusions with the information in the book. Have them write about their comparisons in their journals.

D. Read aloud Chapter 1. Have students discuss how the scientists must have felt discovering totally new life at the bottom of the ocean.

Closure
Have students write in their journals about how plate tectonics affects life in the ocean.

Extensions
Have students use the following Web site to learn more about giant tubeworms.

http://www.ocean.udel.edu/deepsea/level-2/creature/tube.html

Assessment
Assess student journal entries and the conclusions drawn about the information presented in the article.

Discoveries

Touring the Ocean
By O. Shawn Lover

I was recently asked to be a part of an exploration team. The team was asked to study life on the ocean floor. Most of us theorized that nothing could live on the ocean floor. It would be too dark and cold. The extreme water pressure would surely crush a fish trying to live there.

One way we were studying the ocean floor was by dragging a thermometer, with weights of course, near the bottom. This can get fairly boring as the thermometer records temperatures right around 34° F for several days and nights in a row.

We were in the Pacific Ocean off the coast of South America when suddenly someone realized that the temperature had gone up a few degrees. What could have caused the temperature increase?

An Island Is Born
By Icene Newland

Deep under the ocean, scientists have discovered a new island forming. The crust at the bottom of the ocean is thin and scientists have discovered places
.

where boiling hot water and steam rise through cracks. One of these places has magma oozing from the crack. As scientists continue to study the area, the layers of magma cooling continue to get thicker. Scientists predict that it will take several thousand years for the island to reach above the surface of the water.

Strange Fish Washes Ashore
By Fon E. Fenz

Scientists near the coast of Ecuador, South America have found a fish that has never been seen. A local found the fish as he was walking along the beach in Ecuador during the night.

"I saw these strange, tiny lights on the beach ahead of me. I thought a child's toy had washed ashore. When I saw that the lights were coming from the fish, I called my friend who is a biologist to come take a look."

As soon as the scientists saw the fish, they knew nothing like it had ever been discovered. The fish had bioluminescent, or glowing, qualities. Scientists can only guess that the fish must live near the bottom of the ocean and that the light sources on its body are used to attract prey or possibly mates.

Activity 23 – Landforms and Their Causes

Instructional Materials
- books about various landforms such as mountains, the Grand Canyon, geysers, glaciers, caves, etc., and
- a computer with Internet access.

Background Information
When students begin learning about the ocean in the next part of Earth Central, they will learn that the bottom of the ocean has many of the same kinds of **landforms** that occur on land. Many of these landforms do not share the same name. This activity will help students make connections between the inside of the Earth and the outside of the Earth, both above and below the sea.

A. Have students brainstorm different landforms they can see.

B. Have students work in pairs to read about one of the listed landforms. Have them record the following information in their journals:
- the name of the landform,
- where you can see this landform,
- what caused this landform,
- whether this landform caused by things happening inside the Earth or forces on the outside of the Earth,
- whether there are any of these landforms near your town, and
- a picture of this landform.

C. Invite students to present their findings to the class.

Closure
Have students answer the following question in their journals.
How do the inside and the outside of the Earth work together to create the land on which we live?

Extensions
A. Help students use the Internet to discover new islands that have appeared in the past 100 years.

B. Have students select one landform mentioned above to research more in depth. After the research is complete, have students create a large model of the landform using papier-mâché or some other art material.

Assessment
Assess student journal entries and the completed research.

Activity 24 - Learning Ring

Instructional Materials
♦ 1 copy of Ring of Fire Game Cards.

Preparation
Cut out each of the **Ring of Fire Game Cards**. Here is how to play the game:
♦ Give one card to each student in the class. If you have more cards than students, some students will get more than one card.
♦ The student with the smiley face on his or her card reads their card first. In this game, the student will read, "I have geophysics. Who has a mountain caused by magma?"
♦ The student having the card reading, "I have volcano. Who has where magma is stored under a volcano?" would read his or her card next.
♦ Play continues until the answers loop back to the first person's answer.

A. Play the game, and time students to see how fast they can complete the loop.

B. Challenge students to complete the loop faster by playing the game a second time. Pick up the cards and redistribute them so each person receives a different card. Play the game several times, each time recording the time it takes to complete the loop.

Closure
Invite students to discuss the outcome of the game. Ask students to draw conclusions about the number of times the game was played and the amount of time it took to complete each loop.

Extensions
A. Have students form three teams. Challenge each team to develop a Learning Ring game based on what has been learned so far during Earth Central. Make copies of each game before allowing students to cut them apart.

B. Play each game that was created. If there are problems, allow time for students to make revisions.

C. Keep the games in your reference book center. Students can take turns putting the cards in the order of the loop.

Assessment
Assess the conclusions students drew about the time it took to complete the game versus practice. If students completed the Extensions, assess their ability to create their own loop game.

Ring of Fire Game Cards

\I have **geophysics**. Who has a mountain caused by

I have **volcano**. Who has where magma is stored under a volcano?

I have **magma chamber**. Who has a place underground

I have a **sill**. Who has the chimney through which magma rises to

I have the **central vent**. Who has the funnel-shaped opening at the

I have **crater**. Who has the name of the Roman god of fire?

I have **Vulcan**. Who has magma that has reached the surface?

I have **lava**. Who has a volcano that is no longer active?

I have **extinct**. Who has a volcano that is cold, but waiting to erupt?

I have **dormant**. Who has a volcano that spews smoke, ash, and lava?

I have **active**. Who has the area around the Pacific Ocean where

I have **Ring of Fire**. Who has the tallest mountain in the world?

I have **Mauna Kea**. Who has a rock formed by layers of sediment?

I have **sedimentary**. Who has a rock formed by pressure

I have **metamorphic**. Who has a rock formed from magma or lava?

I have **igneous**. Who has a vehicle that can travel underwater?

I have **submersible**. Who has chimneys under the

I have **deep-sea vents**. Who has one who studies how the inside and outside of Earth work together?

I have a **geophysicist**. Who has a group of letters added

I have **prefix**. Who has the name of a word to which a prefix or

I have **root word**. Who has a group of letters added to the end of a root word?

I have **suffix**. Who has the study of how the inside and outside of Earth work together?

Activity 25 – Sea Sort Association

Instructional Materials
♦ 6 copies of **Sea Sort Game Cards,**
♦ several books about the ocean, and
♦ student journals.

Preparation
Cut each set of **Sea Sort Game Cards** apart and place them into separate envelopes. Collect several books about the ocean, tides, currents, hurricanes, etc., and place them in the research center for student use.

A. Have students form six teams. Provide an envelope for each team.

B. Inform teams that there are three categories of words inside each envelope. It is their job to sort the words into the categories. Category headings are in bold print.

C. Allow 15–20 minutes for teams to categorize their words, then invite teams to share how they categorized.

Closure
Distribute journals and have students write to the following prompt:
How do you think all the words from the game apply to Earth?

Extensions

A. Invite students to develop word sort games using different subjects. For example, they could choose three categories such as meat, fruits, and vegetables. Then they could brainstorm words for each category. Have students make word association cards and trade games with other teams.

B. Challenge students to select a category heading or word within a category and create a word web about it. Students should list everything they can about the word in the web. Write the following example on the chalkboard.

How do they form?

Damage
- flooding
- winds
- mud slides

Hurricane names

Hurricanes

Strength categories

Where do they form?

Famous hurricanes

C. Have students research one of the topics in the word webs they created. Provide opportunities for students to share their research with the class.

Assessment

Assess teamwork during the word association task and journal entries during the Closure section.

Sea Sort Game Cards

Ocean Geography	Ocean	Oceans and Weather
seamount	crest	hurricane
volcano	trough	water spout
trench	tsunami	wind
mountain ridge	tides	sea breeze
continental shelf	current	typhoon

Activity 26 – Globe Roll

Instructional Materials
♦ 1 globe,
♦ 1 large world map,
♦ 1 package of sticky notes or sticky dots, and
♦ books about oceans for the research area.

Background Information
The Earth is almost covered with water. Only about one-fourth of the surface of the Earth is land. Large areas of water on Earth are called **oceans**. The largest ocean is the **Pacific** Ocean, which covers about one-third of the Earth's surface. The **Atlantic** is the second-largest ocean, covering one-fifth of Earth's surface. The **Indian** Ocean covers a little less than one-fifth of Earth's surface and is the third-largest ocean. The **Antarctic** and **Arctic** are the fourth- and fifth-largest oceans, respectively, covering about one-eighth of the Earth's surface together. Over 95 percent of Earth's water is located in the oceans.

A. Tell students that the Earth's surface is mostly covered with water. Ask students to share ways they know this is true.

B. Have students form several teams to devise ways to test and prove the hypothesis that the Earth is covered with water. Allow students to use the globe and large map.

C. Invite students to share the ways they devised to test and prove the hypothesis.

D. Have students sit in a circle on the floor. Give each student two sticky notes or two sticky dots. If your globe is on a stand, pass it to each student. Have each student spin the globe and then stop it. Ask students to place a sticky note or dot on the place where their right pinkie fingers touch the globe. If your globe is not on a stand, have students carefully roll the globe across the circle to one another. Each time the globe is rolled, the catcher should place a sticky note or dot on the place where his or her right pinkie finger is touching the globe.

E. Have students tally the number of dots touching land and the number touching water. Then have them construct a bar graph to show the results.

F. Have students determine the ratio of land to ocean using the bar graph. They can determine a percentage by dividing the number of times the dot was touching land by the number of times the dot was touching ocean. For example:

Number of times touching land: 17
Number of times touching ocean: 24

Ratio: $\underline{17}$
          24

Dividing 17 by 24 = 0.708

Percentage: about 71 percent

G. Share the Background Information.

Closure

Have students write to the following prompt in their journals:
Over 70 percent of the Earth is covered in oceans. What conclusions can you draw from this statement?
Sample conclusions: There is very little land on Earth. Most of our water on Earth is not drinkable (due to salt content).

Extensions

A. Invite students to form several teams to research the four major oceans. Encourage them to find the following information:
- How many square miles does the ocean cover?
- How deep is the ocean's deepest point?
- What are some special characteristics of the ocean?

B. Provide a time for students to present their research to the class. If you created a Web site, have students add their ocean research to the site.

Assessment

Assess the experiments devised by students to prove the hypothesis that the Earth is mostly covered in water. Assess journal entries from the Closure section.

Activity 27 - A Tension, Please

Instructional Materials

- ◆ 3 small bowls,
- ◆ 3 pennies,
- ◆ 3 straws,
- ◆ pepper,
- ◆ 3 needles,
- ◆ liquid soap, and
- ◆ 3 copies of **Tension Experiments**.

Background Information

Water has special **properties** that make it different from many other liquids. When we examine a droplet of water, it looks like a tiny half sphere, or **hemisphere**. We can fill a glass of water over the rim because of the **cohesive** properties of water. The water that sticks out above the rim of the glass forms a hemisphere called a **meniscus**. The cohesive property of water is called **surface tension**.

The surface tension of water can be affected in many ways. Chemicals such as oil and soap can affect water's cohesive properties. The less surface tension the water has, the more difficult it is for something to float. For example, ducks depend on surface tension to float. If ducks get into soap or soap gets into their pond, it is difficult for them to remain afloat.

When we do laundry, we add soap to the water. The soap lessens the amount of surface tension. This helps get the dirt out of our clothes and washed away with the water.

A. Have students form three teams. Distribute student journals and **Tension Experiments**. Share the Background Information before beginning experiments.

B. Have students complete the activities on the **Tension Experiments** sheet. Then have them answer the questions at the end of the sheet in their journals.

Closure

Invite students to share their findings from the experiments and the answers to the questions in their journals.

Extensions

A. Have students complete the experiments using different liquids, such as apple juice, soda water, etc. Ask students to determine which liquid had the most surface tension and what research they have to prove their theory.

B. Challenge students to research oil spills and how they affect the oceans. Invite students to share their research with the class.

Assessment

Assess student journal entries and team cooperation during the experiments.

Tension Experiments

Instructional Materials
♦ 1 small bowl,
♦ 1 penny,
♦ water,
♦ 1 straw,
♦ pepper,
♦ 1 needle, and
♦ liquid soap.

Instructions

Part 1: How Many Drops?
1. How many drops of water do you think you can place on a penny without the water spilling off? Predict the number and record that prediction in your journal.

2. Dip a straw into water and place your finger over the other end. This will trap water inside the straw. Begin dropping water onto the penny slowly. Count the drops that stay on the penny.

3. Answer the following questions in your journal:
♦ How many drops of water was the penny able to support?
♦ What was the difference between your estimation and the actual number of drops?
♦ Why was the penny able to hold so many drops of water?

Part 2: Floating Needle
1. Tear a small piece of paper and float it in a bowl of water.

2. Gently place a needle on top of the paper.

3. Slowly push the paper under the water so that it sinks. The needle should float on top of the water without the support of the paper.

4. Answer the following questions in your journal:
♦ Why was the needle able to float on top of the water?
♦ What purpose did the paper serve in the beginning of the experiment?

Part 3: Disturbing the Surface Tension
1. Using the same bowl with the needle floating, sprinkle some pepper on the water. Observe the pepper for one minute. Most of it will float.

2. Add one drop of liquid soap to the bowl.

3. Answer the following questions in your journal:
♦ What happened to the needle when you added soap? Why do you think this happened?
♦ What happened to the pepper when you added soap? Why do you think this happened?
♦ How is soap, a cleaning product, related to surface tension?

Activity 28 - Oh, Great Water Pressure

Instructional Materials
- ♦ (1) 2-liter bottle per team,
- ♦ 1 large baking dish per team,
- ♦ water,
- ♦ student journals, and
- ♦ a computer with Internet access.

Background Information
One of the major reasons that the ocean and space remain unexplored is because of the difficulty traveling in either place. We need special modes of transportation with human life support built in to survive the harsh conditions in each place.

The ocean, like space, provides several **obstacles** for humans to overcome; the most obvious being a lack of breathable air. Humans can't breathe the oxygen in water because we have no gills. A less obvious obstacle for human exploration of the ocean is the tremendous amount of **pressure** the water exerts on any object under the surface. When a person swims deep under the water, the pressure can be felt in the ears and nose. The deepest recorded dive for a human with no special equipment is over 400 feet deep. At this depth, there would be a tremendous amount of pressure on the ears and other parts of the body. It is very dangerous to dive that deep with no equipment.

The farther down you go in the ocean, the more pressure there is. The amount of pressure at the bottom of the ocean would be enough to crush a car. Special submarines have been used to travel to the deepest known parts of the ocean. The deepest area in the ocean, the **Marianas Trench**, is located in the Pacific Ocean near Guam. The Marianas Trench is almost 7 miles below the surface of the water.

A. Have students form three teams. Each team should collect a 2-liter bottle, a large baking dish, and their journals.

B. Have each team poke three holes in their bottles using a sharpened pencil or ballpoint pen at the intervals shown in the illustration.

water pressure, illustrated.

the dish is to contain the mess.

C. Have teams fill their bottles with water. They can recap the bottles and plug the holes with their fingers to get the bottles from the sink to their work areas.

D. Have each team remove the cap and take their fingers off the top hole in the bottle. They should only remove their finger for 2–3 seconds. Then they should re-plug the hole. Have students mark where the water squirted to with a crayon.

E. Instruct students to replace the water that spilled out of the bottles and repeat the experiment with the middle and lowest holes in the bottles. Each time they should mark with a crayon where the water squirted.

F. Have students refill the bottles one last time and unplug all three holes at once. Ask them to observe whether the water squirted to the same places from each hole as before.

Closure

A. Have students answer the following questions in their journals:
♦ Did the water squirt farther from the top hole or bottom hole? Why did this happen?
♦ What conclusions can you draw about swimming at the top of the ocean as compared to swimming at the bottom of the ocean?

B. Share the Background Information. Have students discuss water pressure and its effects on humans.

Extensions

A. Have students use the following Web site to research scuba diving. As always, please preview all sites before allowing students to view them:

http://library.thinkquest.org/28170/2.html

B. Challenge students to produce a report about the history of scuba diving, including the dangers. If students created a Web site, have them publish their research to the site.

Assessment

Evaluate the journal entries from the Closure section and the water pressure discussion.

Activity 29 – Want Salt With That Ocean?

Instructional Materials
♦ salt,
♦ 5 clear plastic cups,
♦ 2 large pitchers,
♦ very hot water,
♦ very cold water, and
♦ red, blue, and yellow food coloring.

Background Information
The oceans contain enough salt to cover all the land on Earth in a layer 500 feet thick. This salt has washed into the ocean over millions of years. The salt comes from the minerals in the soil. The amount of salt content in a liquid is called **salinity**. The ocean has a high salinity.

Density is defined as the mass of an object. **Mass** is the amount of space something occupies. The more salt a body of water contains, the denser it is. This can be shown by **dissolving** salt in hot and cold water. If you add enough salt to water, a paste forms. The water is dense with salt content.

Hardly any plant or animal life is found in or near the Dead Sea. It is the saltiest sea in the world. The density of the water is so great that a person would have a difficult time swimming under the surface.

A. Have students gather around a demonstration table. Ask for four volunteers to do the following:
♦ Pour cold water into a cup, add several spoons of salt, three drops of blue food coloring, and stir.
♦ Pour cold water into another cup, add one drop of blue and three drops of yellow food coloring (to make green), and stir.
♦ Pour hot water into another cup, add two drops of red food coloring, several spoons of salt, and stir.
♦ Pour hot water into another cup, add one drop of red and three drops of yellow food coloring (to make orange), and stir.

B. Demonstrate the density of fresh water vs. salt water using the following steps.
♦ Tilt the empty cup and pour some cold salt water (blue) into it.
♦ Carefully pour some cold fresh water (green) on top of the salt water. Pour slowly to try to avoid mixing the colors.
♦ Next, pour some of the hot salt water (red) into the cup.
♦ Last, pour some of the hot fresh water into the cup.

C. Students should see something like the sample illustration below.

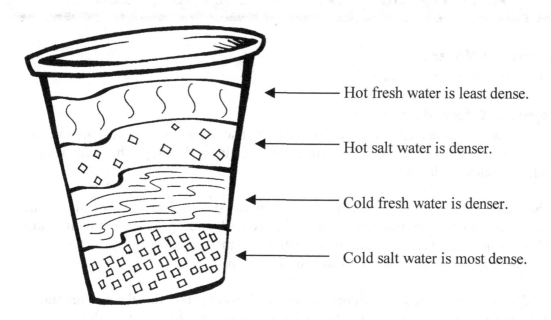

Hot fresh water is least dense.

Hot salt water is denser.

Cold fresh water is denser.

Cold salt water is most dense.

Closure

Have students draw conclusions in their journals about salt water in the oceans. Have them think and write about the following:

♦ the density of the surface ocean water near the mouth of the Mississippi River in the Gulf of Mexico,
♦ the density of the surface ocean water near Brazil in South America, and
♦ the density of the water near the bottom of the ocean around Antarctica.

Possible conclusions:

The ocean water in the Gulf of Mexico would be some of the least dense in the ocean, being a mixture of warm fresh water and salt water. The ocean water near Brazil would be less dense because it is warmer. The ocean water under Antarctica would be the densest because of its temperature.

Extension

Remind students that water, especially fresh water, is a precious resource. Have students research techniques to convert salt water into fresh water. Ask students to report on the cost and likelihood that it will ever be done. Ask students to discuss why it is important to conserve water.

Assessment

Assess the Closure activity by reviewing students' conclusions.

Activity 30 – Ocean Geography 101

Instructional Materials

◆ computer with Internet access.

Background Information

Every continent is connected to the crust of the Earth and to one or more vast oceans. Just as the continents have unique landforms such as mountains and valleys, the ocean floor has unique features of its own.

The **shoreline** is where the continents and oceans meet. At some beaches a swimmer can wade out into the water for 100 yards or more before finding deep water. The **continental shelf** begins out past where you can't touch bottom anymore. The water where the continental shelf begins is between 50 and 100 feet deep.

Eventually the slope of the ocean floor gets steeper. This area is called the **continental slope**. Near the bottom of the ocean, the continent is connected to the ocean floor by the **continental rise**. The flat plains that cover the majority of the ocean floor are called the **abyssal plains**. The abyssal plains are covered in sand, mud, and the remains of plants and ocean creatures. Sometimes this muddy bottom can be over 5,000 feet thick.

The ocean floor isn't totally flat. There are mountains called **seamounts**. Long lines of seamounts are called **mountain ridges**. In some areas where the ocean floor is spreading apart due to plate tectonics, deep **trenches** are formed. Some mountains that occur underwater have flat tops. These mountains are called **guyots**. Valleys between mountain ridges are called **rift valleys**.

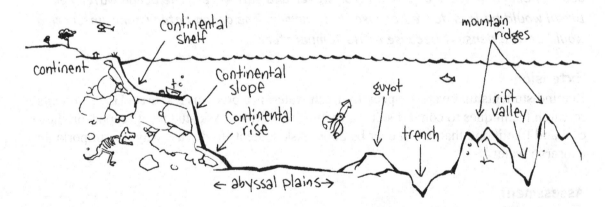

A. Share the Background Information and discuss how the geography of the ocean floor is similar to the geography of Earth's surface.

B. Have students list the bolded vocabulary words in the Background Information. Then have them brainstorm similar land features.
Possible responses:

Ocean Feature	Land Feature
shoreline	beach
seamount	mountain
mountain ridge	mountain range
trench	canyon
guyot	plateau
rift valley	valley

C. Challenge students to develop a game to help them learn the names and definitions of the geographical features on the ocean floor. Suggestions include crossword puzzles, concentration games, word matches, or spelling bees.

D. Have students form six teams. Each team should devise a game to learn the geography of the ocean floor. Be sure students write instructions for their games. If teams create crossword puzzles, make copies of each puzzle or laminate them so they can be erased and reworked.

E. Allow students to present and teach their games to other students. Have students trade games with one another.

F. Place the completed games in the research area of your classroom.

Closure

Have students write a paragraph in their journals telling how the geography of the ocean floor is similar to and different from the geography of Earth's surface.

Extensions

A. If you created a Web site, have students publish their games to the site. The games don't have to be interactive, or played on the computer. Have students publish the games in such a way that they can be printed and copied for others to play.

B. Have students ask permission to take their games to another class. Students should devise a geography lesson to teach the class before showing them how to play the games.

Assessment

Assess the journal entries from the Closure activity.

Activity 31 - Tour the Ocean

Instructional Materials
♦ *The Magic School Bus on the Ocean Floor* book, by Joanna Cole;
♦ 2 large sheets of butcher paper;
♦ art supplies; and
♦ a computer with Internet access.

Background Information
The Magic School Bus series does a wonderful job of teaching science concepts regarding the oceans, weather, and space. As you read, be sure to share the notes to the side of the main text.

A. Select several students to take turns reading aloud *The Magic School Bus on the Ocean Floor*. If necessary, remind students to read the notes on the side of each page.

B. After reading, have students discuss whether the book was fiction or nonfiction. Have them list reasons and clues on the chalkboard to prove their thinking.

C. Have students turn to the page near the back of the book showing the picture of the ocean floor mural created by Ms. Frizzle's class. Read through the labels on the mural.

D. Challenge students to create an ocean floor **mural** using butcher paper and art supplies. Use the Background Information from Activity 30 and the book as references. Remind students to label all geographic features on the ocean floor.

Closure
Have students form six teams. Ask teams to determine the main idea of the book. Then have teams discuss how ocean creatures depend on the geography of the ocean to survive.

Extensions
A. Invite another class to see the ocean floor mural. Encourage each student to write a speaking part showing one part of the mural.

B. Take digital pictures of the ocean floor mural and publish the speaking parts from above. Add the information to the Web site.

Assessment
Assess the Closure discussion and ocean floor mural.

Activity 32 – From the Continent to the Abyss

Instructional Materials
♦ copies (or transparency) of **Ocean Song**.

A. Hand out copies of **Ocean Song** or place a transparency on the overhead.

B. Be sure students know the tune, then sing the song.

Closure
Distribute student journals and have students draw **diagrams** of the bottom of the ocean using the words in the song to help them remember.

Extensions
A. Invite another class to hear students sing the song.

B. Challenge students to write other songs about the ocean. Get students started by having them brainstorm the titles of many familiar tunes, such as "Are You Sleeping?" Then have them change the words to create new songs.

Assessment
Assess the ocean floor diagrams.

Ocean Song

(sung to the tune of "Battle Hymn of the Republic")

I'd like to tell the story of the churning of the sea.
I'm a lucky starfish; this is where I like to be.
I live near the seashore, in a big tide pool so green.
Now let me tell you about the sea!

Continental shelf touches the beach.
Continental slope goes very deep!
Continental rise goes even deeper!
Abyssal plains at the bottom of the sea!

Mountain ridges stretch for miles 'neath the surface of the sea.
Areas between them are called ri-ft val-leys.
Guyots are flat-topped mountains that I have never seen.
And trenches, the deepest parts of the sea.

Continental shelf touches the beach.
Continental slope goes very deep!
Continental rise goes even deeper!
Abyssal plains at the bottom of the sea!

Activity 33 - Hit the Waves, Dude!

Instructional Materials
♦ student journals,
♦ rulers,
♦ 1 transparent glass baking dish,
♦ water,
♦ blue food coloring,
♦ computer with Internet access,

Optional:
♦ (1) 2-liter bottle with labels removed,
♦ 1 bottle of rubbing alcohol, and
♦ 1 bottle of baby oil.

Background Information
A **wave** is a rise and fall of ocean water as energy is transferred from one place to another. As the wave gets closer to shore, the bottom starts to drag along the ocean floor. As this happens the bottom of the wave starts to slow down, but the top of the wave keeps moving forward. It gets so far ahead that it falls over and **breaks** onto the beach.

Waves have different sizes and strengths. They can be created by wind, earthquakes, volcanoes, and tides. Most waves are caused by wind pulling and pushing the surface of the ocean. The wind's speed, how long it blows, and how far it blows affect the power and size of waves. The top of the wave is called the **crest**. The bottom is called the **trough**. The distance between one crest to the next crest or from one trough to the next trough is the **wavelength**.

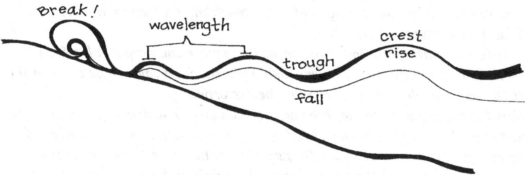

A. Share and discuss the Background Information.

B. Have students make a human wave to learn the parts of a wave.
♦ Ask students to join hands in a circle, then show them how to create a human wave by lifting and lowering one arm at a time.
♦ Only two students should have their arms raised at one time. Once one pair of arms is raised and lowered, the next pair of arms should be raised and lowered.

♦ Have students discuss how the wave moves around the circle.
♦ Ask students to recall the vocabulary for the top and bottom of a wave (crest and trough) and the distance between each wave (wavelength).

C. Distribute student journals and have students draw a diagram of a set of waves, including the crest, trough, wavelength, and a wave breaking on the shore.

D. Draw the following waves on a transparency. Have students come up and measure the wavelengths using a ruler. Ask students the following questions:
♦ Which waves would most likely be closer to shore? Why? (The second set of waves is probably closer to shore because the waves are closer together and moving faster.)
♦ Which waves would most likely be farther from shore? Why? (The first waves are not close to shore because they are farther apart and not moving very quickly.)

E. Set up a wave demonstration on the overhead projector using the baking dish filled three-fourths full of water. Use the following steps for the demonstration:
♦ *Place the baking dish on the overhead and wait for the water to stop moving. Explain that water in the ocean is never perfectly still. There are always waves and currents moving it about.*
♦ *Touch the center of the water with your finger. Have students draw a picture of what happened to the water when it was disturbed. Ask students to identify what caused the waves. (your finger touching the surface of the water) Ask students to identify something that could touch the surface of the ocean to make it have waves. (wind)*
♦ *Wait for the water to stop moving again. Then place one drop of blue food coloring in the middle of the baking dish. Hold the food coloring as close to the surface as possible so the water won't be disturbed.*
♦ *Wait for the water to settle, then drop a solid object such as a penny into the center of the baking dish. Have students draw a picture of the movement of waves from the center outward. Be sure they notice that the waves travel outward until reaching the walls of the baking dish, and are reflected back toward the center.*

Closure

Have students answer the following questions in their journals:
♦ How do waves affect the surface of the ocean?
♦ How do waves affect the shoreline?
♦ List several outside forces that cause waves.
♦ How does the information about earthquakes and volcanoes presented during earlier activities in Earth Central help you understand how tsunamis form?
♦ What has to happen in the ocean for a tsunami to form?

Extensions

A. Have students research tsunamis using the following Web sites. As always, please preview the sites before allowing students to view them.

http://www.germantown.k12.il.us/html/tsunami.html
http://www.fema.gov/library/tsunami.htm

B. Challenge students to prepare a presentation about waves. They should include a demonstration about how they form, wave vocabulary, and the destruction caused by tsunamis. The presentation can be given to another class.

C. If your class has produced a Web site, have them take digital pictures of the presentation and add the information to the site.

D. Have students make a wave in a bottle using **Wave in a Bottle**.

Assessment

Evaluate the journal entries in the Closure activity.

Wave in a Bottle

Instructional Materials
- ♦ (1) 2-liter bottle with labels removed,
- ♦ 1 bottle of rubbing alcohol,
- ♦ 1 bottle of baby oil, and
- ♦ blue food coloring.

Instructions:
1. Drop 5–7 drops of blue food coloring into the empty 2-liter bottle.

2. Fill the bottle half full with rubbing alcohol. Replace the cap and shake well to mix the food coloring and alcohol.

3. Remove the cap again, tilt the bottle, and fill the remainder of the bottle with baby oil. Fill the bottle completely so no air remains in the bottle. Replace the cap on the bottle tightly.

4. Tilt the bottle gently to see the waves.

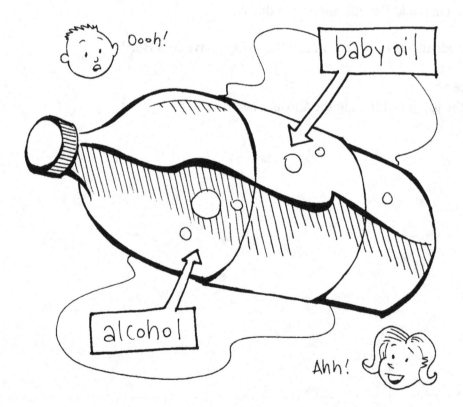

Activity 34 – In and Out With the Tide

Instructional Materials
♦ student journals,
♦ 1 wire hanger per student,
♦ 1 copy of **Tide Mobile**, **Tide 1**, **Tide 2**, and **Tide Mobile Patterns** for each student, and
♦ yarn.

Background Information
The ocean is always moving. Motion is affected by winds, underwater activity such as volcanoes, and currents in the deepest parts of the sea. The motion of the water is also affected by **astrological** forces, the moon and the sun.

There are two basic kinds of tides. There is the **high tide**, also known as **flood tide**. And there is **low tide**, which is also called **ebb tide**. High tide and low tide each occur once a day, though they can occur twice in parts of the world. These tides are caused by the **gravitational** pull of the sun and the moon. Although the sun is bigger, the moon has more effect on the tides because it is closer.

During low tide, crevices and pools along beaches remain full of water. These are called **tide pools**, and they are home to a variety of ocean life. Some animals are carried in and out with the tides. Creatures living in tide pools include sea anemones, starfish, sand dollars, crabs, and tiny fish.

A. Ask students to solve the following riddles:
♦ I am covered in water and land. Each day and night, the water on me is affected by the sun and moon. What am I? (Earth)
♦ I orbit Earth every 24 hours. My gravitational pull causes the oceans to follow me wherever I go. What am I? (the moon)
♦ Earth orbits me every 365 days. My gravitational pull has an effect on the oceans, but not as much as the moon. What am I? (the sun)
♦ Sometimes the ocean is high on me and sometimes it is low. What am I? (the beach or the shore)
♦ When the moon pulls the ocean toward the beach you see me. What am I? (high tide)
♦ When the moon is out of sight and the ocean is not pulled toward the beach you see me. What am I? (low tide)

B. Share the Background Information about tides, then have a teams demonstrate how the tides work using their bodies. Have students form teams of five and assign students in each team to the following parts: sun, beach, moon, high tide, low tide. Encourage teams to be creative in their presentations. They may create a song to go with their presentations.

C. Invite teams to demonstrate how high tide and low tide occur on the beach.

D. Have students use **Tide Mobile**, **Tide 1**, **Tide 2**, and **Tide Mobile Patterns** to create a tide mobile.

Closure

Have students write an explanation of tides and how they affect Earth. Allow time for peer editing, then have students print a final copy on a computer. Have students hang their tide mobiles in the room or a hallway. Students should hang their writing under their mobiles.

Extensions

A. Challenge students to develop a play with speaking parts and songs to explain tides to a class of younger students.

B. Have students ask permission to perform the play for other classes. Then allow time for tide play performances.

Assessment

Assess the writing during the Closure activity.

Tide Mobile

Instructional Materials
- 1 wire hanger per student,
- yarn (blue or black),
- crayons or markers,
- tape,
- ruler,
- scissors, and
- glue.

Instructions

1. Color and cut out **Tide 1** and **Tide 2**. Assemble the two tides by gluing the pieces together. One side represents high tide and the other represents low tide. Color the waves on each side with crayons.

2. Cut out the rhyme on **Tide Mobile Patterns** and glue it to the back of the tide.

3. Attach the tide to the hanger using blue yarn. Follow the illustration below. The high tide should hang 5 inches below the base of the hanger. Make sure the tides hang evenly.

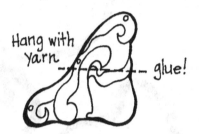

4. Color and cut the other patterns on **Tide Mobile Patterns**. Color the moon and tape it above the high tide on the correct corner of the hanger. Color the sun and clouds and hang them, with yarn, above the low tide. The sun and clouds should balance the mobile. If it is not balanced, create another item to hang with the sun. Maybe a shell or a starfish that you might find at low tide.

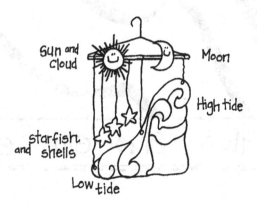

Tide 1

Instructions: Cut out **Tide 1** and attach it to **Tide 2**. Hang the high and low tide from the clothes hanger as instructed.

Glue··· Glue··· Glue··· Glue··· Glue

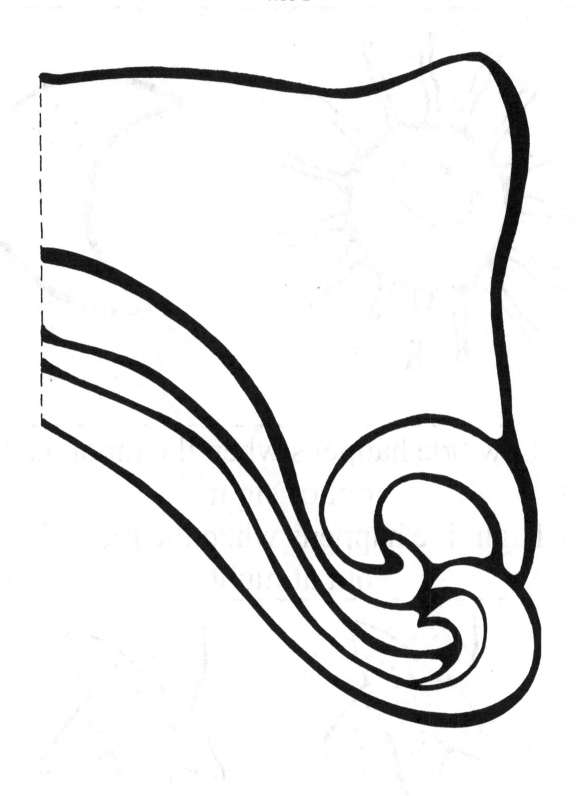

Low tide happens when the moon is
out of sight.
High tide happens when the moon is
out at night.

Instructional Materials

♦ student journals.

Background Information

A wave is not like a current. **Currents** move water from one place to another. They are like giant rivers in the ocean. You cannot see currents from the surface of the ocean. Oceanographers must measure the motion of the water underneath the sea to find currents. A wave is visible from the surface, but a wave is not moving water.

Currents are caused by wind and temperature changes. Look at the diagram below. If the Earth is divided into the northern and southern hemispheres, you can see that the currents in the northern hemisphere move in a counterclockwise rotation. The currents in the southern hemisphere move in a clockwise rotation. These currents are affected by **prevailing winds**. Prevailing winds blow mostly in one direction over a certain area. These currents are also affected by the frigid waters near Antarctica and the North Pole. The currents in Earth's oceans take warmer water toward the **polar regions** and cooler water toward the **equator**. This, in a sense, is the way Earth regulates its temperatures, like using air-conditioning and heat. Currents affect Earth's climate and weather.

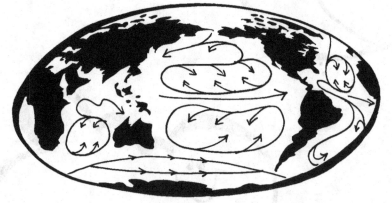

A. Share the Background Information. Ask half of the students to stand and form a circle in the south half of the room. Tell the other students to form a circle in the north half.

B. Remind students that currents in the northern hemisphere move in a counterclockwise rotation and the opposite in the southern hemisphere. Have students simulate currents in the northern and southern hemispheres by walking in a circle.

C. Ask students to predict what weather conditions would be like where the two currents and two prevailing winds meet. (It would probably be windy.) Ask students to predict the temperatures in the area where the two currents meet. (The area is near the equator, so it would be warm, if not hot, and humid.)

D. Ask students to predict what happens when a warm, humid, windy air mass meets a cooler air mass. (Storms develop.) Tell students they will be learning more about the development of storms in the next several activities.

Closure

Have students answer the following questions in their journals.
♦ How are currents formed?
♦ How are currents affected by the wind?
♦ How do currents affect our weather?

Extension

Invite students to research the Gulf Stream. At nearly 40 miles wide and about 2,000 miles long, it is one of the largest currents on Earth.

Assessment

Assess the journal entries from the Closure activity.

Activity 36 – Build a Weather Station

Instructional Materials
- several books about weather, storms, water cycle, etc.;
- 1 large sheet of butcher paper;
- 3 Wild Wacky Weather kits from The Wild Goose Company;
- 1 hair dryer;
- water;
- 4 adult volunteers;
- 1 current newspaper;
- student journals;

Optional
- 1 outdoor thermometer; and
- 1 rain gauge.

Background Information
Forecasting the weather has been a human passion for ages. Farmers wanted to know what kind of a season was coming. Would there be enough rain or would there be drought? Would the winter be cold or mild? How could they tell if a violent storm was coming? Before TV, weather reports, or Doppler radar, people relied on natural signs to help them predict the weather.

The study of weather began many centuries ago with a scientist named **Aristotle**. Aristotle lived in ancient Greece about 340 B.C. He studied the weather and the **climate**. (Climate is defined as the weather over a period of time.) Back then, anything that fell from the sky (rain or snow) or anything that was in the sky (like clouds) was called a meteor. The term meteor comes from the Greek word *meteoros*, which means "high in the sky." This is how meteorology got its name.

Meteorology today is the study of Earth's atmosphere and weather. Meteorologists specialize in studying weather and its changes. They study the air composition, temperature, pressure, wind speed, direction, precipitation, and humidity. They also study clouds, weather systems, seasons, hurricanes, tornadoes, and even rainbows. All of this is controlled by the sun and the tilt of the Earth on its axis. Meteorologists watch for anything falling from the sky or floating around in it. Thanks to modern science, meteorologists don't just have to rely on their senses anymore. From wind vanes to space satellites, the weather is watched with hundreds of instruments around the globe.

Preparation
Gather several books about weather, storms, and the water cycle and place them in your research center for students to use throughout their study of weather.
Read through the following activities in the Wild Wacky Weather booklet:

- ◆ Monsoon Measure, page 11;
- ◆ Take the Pressure, page 16;
- ◆ Rooster Booster, page 20; and
- ◆ Speedy Breezolas, page 23.

Decide which weather instruments your class will make before beginning the activity. Enlist the help of several parent volunteers to monitor and aid teams as needed.

Create a weather observation chart like the one below. Be sure to include only the observations students will be making. For example, if you choose not to make the Speedy Breezolas to measure wind speed, then don't include wind speed on the chart.

Today is...	Temperature	Wind Speed/ Direction	Rain	Humidity	Barometric Pressure
Monday					
Tuesday					
Wednesday					
Thursday					
Friday					
Monday					
Tuesday					
Wednesday					
Thursday					
Friday					

A. Tell students they will be building a weather observation station.

B. Have students form three teams. Each team will make one of the following weather observation tools:
- ◆ Monsoon Measure, page 11;
- ◆ Take the Pressure, page 16;
- ◆ Rooster Booster, page 20; and
- ◆ Speedy Breezolas, page 23.

C. Provide each team a Wild Wacky Weather kit and booklet and a parent volunteer. Have teams work to create their own weather instruments.

D. Take the new measurement instruments outside and have each team demonstrate them. The hygrometer should be placed in a sheltered spot outside where it won't be disturbed by sun, wind, or rain. The same is true for the barometer. The thermometer (if you collected one) should be placed in an open, shaded area. The rain gauge (if applicable) should be placed in an open area. The wind vane and wind speed instruments can be taken out and brought in daily.

E. Have students take temperature and wind readings for the first day. For each day after that, readings should be taken for all weather instruments.

F. Have students draw a chart in their journals like the one in the Preparation section. Have students use the information on the class chart to forecast the next day's weather.

Closure
Have students look at the weather forecast in the newspaper and discuss it.

Extensions
A. Have students write a paper explaining how they made and used their weather instruments. Then have them write an explanation of how their instruments work.

B. If you created a Web site, have students publish their how-to papers to the Web site. Take digital pictures to include in the Web site.

Assessment
Assess the weather instruments and the writing from the Closure activity.

Activity 37 – Round and Round

Instructional Materials
♦ weather chart from Activity 36,
♦ student journals,
♦ metal cake or sheet pan,
♦ hot tap water,
♦ ice cubes,
♦ large glass jar, and
♦ computer with Internet access.

Background Information
Every day when the sun comes out it heats the surface of the Earth, beginning a process called **evaporation**. Puddles, lakes, oceans, even the dew on plants, evaporate. Evaporation is the process of a liquid changing into a gas. When heated by the sun, water breaks down into tiny **molecules** that float into the air. We call this gas **water vapor**. The water vapor rises to the cooler air above. As it cools, the water vapor collects together around other particles floating in the air. These particles can be specs of dust, salt, or even small bugs. This collection of water molecules forms a cloud in a process called **condensation**. As the water vapor continues to condense, the cloud gets larger and heavier. The water vapor molecules bond together until they are too heavy to remain in the cloud and fall back to the ground in the form of rain. This is called **precipitation**. Then the cycle begins again.

Preparation
Prepare ice cubes before class. Locate an area large enough to play Let's Precipitate. Locate an area tall enough to measure 6-feet-7-inches in height. Locate a step stool or chair (for your use only).

A. Have students complete the weather chart for the day. Compare the current weather to yesterday's predictions.

B. Share the Background Information.

C. Share the following dialogue with the class: Most of our rainwater comes from the oceans. What is the ocean nearest you called? Imagine that every year 79 inches of that ocean evaporated. How tall is that? (Remind students to divide 79 by 12 to find height in feet. Ask for a student volunteer to go to the chalkboard and demonstrate how to divide the two numbers. The answer is 6, remainder 7, or 6-feet-7 inches.) Have students use a ruler or yardstick and masking tape to mark the height on the wall of your classroom.

D. Ask students the following question: Have you ever swam in the deep end of a pool? Some deep ends are 6 feet or deeper. This can give you an idea of the amount that evaporates from the surface of the oceans. Have students predict whether oceans lose water. (They do, but the supply is replenished by rainstorms and runoff from the land.) Ask students to share how the water returns to the oceans (through runoff produced by rainstorms on land).

E. Ask for volunteers to perform the experiment on **Indoor Clouds**.

Closure
In their journals, have students answer the following questions:
♦   How does the Indoor Clouds experiment relate to the water cycle?
♦   How does the Indoor Clouds experiment relate to weather?
♦   Where else have you ever noticed condensation?
♦   What conclusions can you draw about the water cycle from the experiment?
♦   How does the ocean affect all the weather on Earth?

Extensions
A. Challenge students to write a song that teaches about the water cycle. Tell them to be sure to use the words *evaporation*, *condensation*, and *precipitation*.

B. Ask permission for your students to teach their song to another class.

Assessment
Assess the writing in the Closure activity.

Indoor Clouds

Instructional Materials
♦ metal cake or sheet pan,
♦ hot tap water,
♦ ice cubes, and
♦ large glass jar .

Instructions

1. Fill a metal cake pan with ice. Wait a few minutes until the pan gets cold.

2. Pour 2–3 inches of hot tap water into a large glass jar. (Only the teacher may perform this step.)

3. Set the pan of ice on the jar rim and watch what happens.

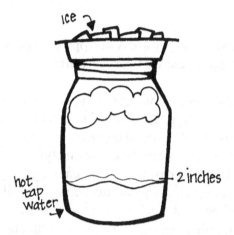

The hot tap water will evaporate, causing water vapor to fill the jar. When the air rises it will run into the cool air at the top of the jar from the metal pan. The cool air will cause the water vapor to condense on the side of the jar and the bottom of the pan.

Activity 38 - Swirling and Whirling Weather

Instructional Materials
- weather chart from Activity 36,
- *The Magic School Bus Inside a Hurricane* book, by Joanna Cole,
- 1 bowl filled with water,
- 1 small piece of Styrofoam,
- 1 glass of water,
- 3 copies of **Hurricane in a Bowl,**
- 3 copies of **Hurricane Movie Magic,**
- 3 medium boxes,
- 6 paper towel rolls,
- white, unlined paper, and
- a computer with Internet access.

Background Information
Hurricanes are large spinning storms over areas of tropical waters. They are called **typhoons** in the Pacific Ocean and **cyclones** near Australia.

Hurricanes usually form over the warmest waters in the ocean, located near the **equator**. They are most prevalent during the summer months but can occur as late as November. They begin as **tropical depressions**. A tropical depression is an area of low barometric pressure with wind speeds over 38 miles per hour. Storms typically develop around low-pressure areas. The sun heats the surface of the ocean, causing evaporation, and the water vapor condenses into large storm clouds. The storms begin to swirl in a counterclockwise rotation in the northern hemisphere and clockwise in the southern hemisphere. As wind speed increases, it becomes a **tropical storm**. A tropical storm has wind speeds up to 73 miles per hour and can cause mild wind damage and major flood damage. A storm becomes a hurricane if it reaches wind speeds of 74 miles per hour. Hurricanes can create a path of damage over 400 miles wide. They cause high waves and extremely high tides, so flooding damage is always a possibility.

A hurricane is a large spinning area of storms. Lines of storms swirl on the outer edge of the hurricane and form **squall lines**. Winds in the squall lines blow about 40 miles per hour in a medium-size hurricane. The **eye wall** surrounds the center of a hurricane. Here the winds are most powerful, from 74 miles per hour in a minimal hurricane to over 150 miles per hour in a powerful hurricane. The center of a hurricane is called the **eye**. Winds are calm and there is no rain inside the eye. Sometimes birds are trapped in the eye for days as a hurricane can be up to 10 miles high.

A. Have students complete the weather chart for the day. Compare the current weather to yesterday's predictions.

B. Help students visit the following Web site to learn more about hurricanes and to watch a video about how hurricanes develop. As always, please preview the site before allowing student access.

http://www.brainpop.com/science/weather/hurricanes

C. Ask for several volunteers to read *The Magic School Bus Inside a Hurricane* aloud. Ask the following questions after reading.
◆ What was the main idea of the book?
◆ What should you do if you know you're in the path of a hurricane?
◆ How are hurricanes, waves, and tides related?
◆ How are hurricanes affected by the sun?

D. Select several students to perform the hurricane experiment on **Hurricane in a Bowl**. Share the Background Information

E. Have students form three teams. Using the information in the Background, the book, and the Web site accessed in Step B, have students create a rolling movie that describes the development of a hurricane. Use the instructions on **Hurricane Movie Magic**.

Closure
Invite teams to share their hurricane movies with the class.

Extensions
A. Invite students to research famous hurricanes. Start with the Web sites below, then research others. As always, please preview each site before allowing student access.
◆ Read about the 1900 Galveston hurricane at the following site:
http://www.pbs.org/wgbh/amex/1900/peopleevents/pande27.html
◆ Read about Hurricane Grace, also called "The Perfect Storm" from 1991:
http://lwf.ncdc.noaa.gov/oa/satellite/satelliteseye/cyclones/pfctstorm91/pfctstorm.html

B. Add information about hurricanes, digital pictures of hurricane movies, and procedures and pictures of the bowl experiment to the Web site.

Assessment
Assess hurricane movies and the answers and discussion from the book.

Hurricane in a Bowl

Instructional Materials
♦ 1 small piece of Styrofoam,
♦ 1 large round bowl,
♦ 1 glass, and
♦ water.

Instructions
1. Fill a large round bowl half full of water.

2. Ask a student to begin swirling the water in a circle. The student should circle to the left. (Remind students that in the northern hemisphere hurricanes go counterclockwise.)

3. Have the student remove his or her hand when the water is swirling evenly.

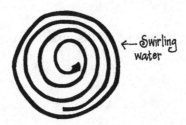

4. Have another student pour a glass of water into the eye, or middle of your hurricane.

5. Ask for observations while this is happening.

6. Have another student place the small piece of Styrofoam on top of the eye, then ask for more observations.

7. Where is the water spinning faster? Where is the water spinning slower? Based on this evidence, draw conclusions about the most destructive part of a hurricane. Record your conclusions in your journal.

Hurricane Movie Magic

Instructional Materials
- 3 medium boxes,
- 6 paper towel rolls,
- white, unlined paper, and
- tape.

Instructions

1. Assign each person on the team one picture to draw, such as evaporation and a small storm over the ocean, a small tropical depression, heavy winds and rain in a tropical storm, high winds and heavy rain in a large hurricane, and the hurricane striking land. Note: everyone should draw their pictures with the paper horizontal on the table.

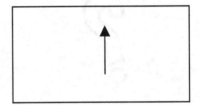

2. After each team member has drawn and colored his or her picture, they should write a paragraph at the bottom describing this point in the development of a hurricane.

3. When all pictures are finished, the team should create a title page and a credits page. The title page should have the title and a picture that summarizes the presentation. The credits page should have every team member's name.

4. Tape all of the pages together in order from left to right so that the title page is the farthest left and the credits page is farthest to the right.

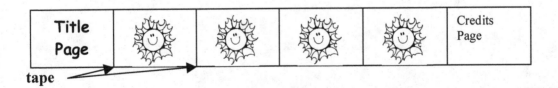

5. Remove the lid from the box. Cut two holes in the long side of each box, about 9 inches wide.

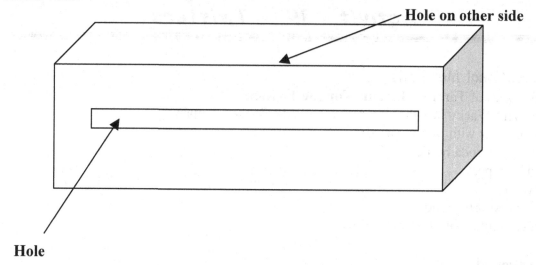

Hole on other side

Hole

6. Facing the opening of the box toward you, slide the title page through the hole on the right side and then through the hole on the left side.

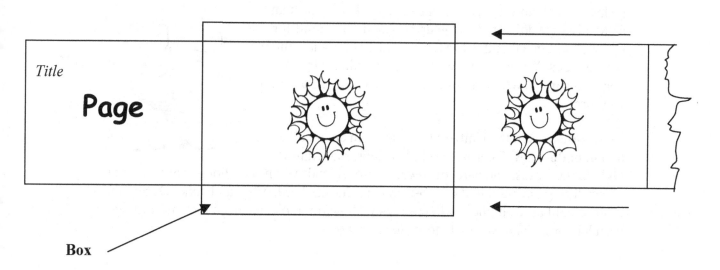

Title

Page

Box

7. Tape each end of the movie strip to a paper towel roll. Roll the end with the credits so the title page is showing in your box movie viewer.

8. "Play" the movie by rolling up the side with the title page and unrolling the side with the credits page. Read the paragraph at the bottom of each page as you roll the movie.

Activity 39 - Twisters

Instructional Materials
- 3 copies of **Terribly Terrific Tongue Twisters**,
- 3 Wild Wacky Weather kits from the Wild Goose Company,
- computer with Internet access,
- 6 plastic soda bottles (2-liter),
- clear tape,
- water,
- food coloring, and
- a computer with Internet access.

Background
Almost all the **tornadoes** occur in the United States. Every state has been hit by at least one. Tornadoes form during thunderstorms, when warm air and cold air clash to form **updrafts** and **downdrafts**. Updrafts are areas of air that suddenly rush upward. Downdrafts are pockets of air that suddenly rush downward. One updraft and downdraft form one **cell** within a thunderstorm. A thunderstorm can contain several cells. When several cells come together they can begin to **rotate**. When the storm begins to rotate, a tornado can form.

Most tornadoes in the United States occur in an area known as **Tornado Alley**. This area includes Nebraska, Kansas, Oklahoma, Texas, and parts of Iowa, Missouri, and Arkansas. Though tornadoes can occur during any month, they mostly occur during April, May, and June. During these months cold air from the North collides with warm, moist air from the south and giant thunderstorms that can create tornadoes are born.

A. Share the Background Information. Ask students to share their experiences with thunderstorms and tornadoes.

B. Tell students they will be participating in two labs. Explain the labs using the following information:

Lab 1—Midwest Connection activity from Wild Goose. See page 34 of Wild Wacky Weather for instructions.

Lab 2—Terribly Terrific Tongue Twisters. Students will practice saying familiar tongue twisters and compose their own. Students should use Terribly Terrific Tongue Twisters to complete this activity. Students should be prepared to share their tongue twisters with the class.

C. Direct students to their lab groups. You should supervise the tornado bottle lab and help with instructions if necessary. Students in the other lab will practice and write tongue twisters. Allow 30–40 minutes before rotating students.

Closure
A. Ask students to share their tornado bottles and tongue twisters with the class.

B. Have students discuss how tornadoes are related to thunderstorms, wind currents, oceans, and the Earth's surface. Create a large chart with student observations and connections between tornadoes and thunderstorms, wind currents, oceans, and the Earth's surface.

Extensions
A. Review your classroom procedure for disaster or tornado drills. Have the class practice getting into correct tornado position.

B. Visit the following Web sites about tornadoes. As always, please view the sites before allowing students to view them.
♦ View storms from the National Severe Storms Laboratory Album:
http://www.photolib.noaa.gov/nssl/tornado1.html
♦ Read actual accounts about tornadoes and see some great pictures, too:
http://whyfiles.news.wisc.edu/013tornado/index.html
Go to this site to learn what the National Oceanic and Atmospheric Administration has to say about tornadoes, how they form, and what we can do to be prepared for them:
http://www.nssl.noaa.gov/NWSTornado/
♦ Visit the following Discovery Channel Web site to read the journal of a stormchaser.
http://www.discovery.com/area/science/tornado/tornado.html

C. Have students research the latest Doppler radar technology and the average time between a tornado warning and the tornado being reported on the ground. Ask students to determine what meteorologists are doing to improve detection equipment of the future.

Assessment
Evaluate the tongue twisters and summaries from the Closure activity.

Terribly Terrific Tongue Twisters

1. Read the following familiar tongue twisters with your lab group. Challenge one another to say them quickly.

She sells seashells on the seashore.

Mommy made me mash my M&M's.

Peter Piper picked a peck of pickled peppers.

2. What other familiar tongue twisters can you think of? Write them in the space below and then practice saying them.

3. Write your own tongue twisters below. Practice saying them as a group and be prepared to share your tongue twisters with the class.

Activity 40 - What Affects the Weather?

Instructional Materials
♦ computer with Internet access, and
♦ 3 copies of **In the News**.

Background Information
The side effects of volcanic eruptions can be as devastating as the blast itself. Volcanic eruptions can occur with earthquakes and affect the weather.

When a volcano erupts, it sends clouds of ash and possibly magma into the air. The pressure of the explosion can send volcanic ash several miles into the air. There the ash is picked up by a **jet stream**. A jet stream is a prevailing wind that blows in the upper atmosphere of Earth. The ash from the Mount St. Helens eruption in 1980 was carried all around the world in the wind. Ash was deposited all over North America.

The amount of ash sent into the sky by a volcano can block the sun's rays and cool temperatures slightly, according to scientific data.

A. Have students form three teams. Provide each team with a copy of **In the News**. Have students read the articles and use the scientific method posters to hypothesize, predict, and draw conclusions based on the observations in the articles. Have students record in their journals a hypothesis, a prediction and a conclusion about each article.

B. Have students share their hypotheses, predictions, and conclusions. Discuss each set of conclusions and the likelihood of each before moving on.

C. Share the Background Information. Discuss what other natural elements can affect the weather. (Large asteroids hitting Earth can cause large amounts of dust to travel into the atmosphere; huge dust storms; etc.)

Closure
Invite students to discuss how weather can be affected by the inside of the Earth and the ocean.

Extension
Have students research famous volcanic eruptions and their effects the eruptions had on weather around the globe.

Assessment
Assess the journal entries and Closure discussion.

© Prufrock Press Inc.

In the News

The Sky is Falling!

By Raine E. Mudd

During a recent thunderstorm, several residents in Mexico reported mud falling from the sky.

Homes were covered in drops of mud. Cars that were clean before the storm were covered in gray mud right after the storm.

Scientists are puzzled. They have seen rain, sleet, snow, and hail fall from the sky, but never mud. Where could the mud have come from?

Rivers of Mud

By Flo Tindirt

As mud was pouring from the sky in one part of Mexico, mud was flowing down the river in another part.

Residents reported feeling a slight earthquake. Then the water in the river became cloudy and then turned to a thick, running mud after a few minutes.

Because the river had so much mud, it overflowed its banks and caused extensive flooding. Many homes were lost or severely damaged.

Farm animals unable to move from their pens were lost as well. Scientists don't know what to make of the river of mud.

Temperatures Mild for Summer

By Cool N. Down

Meteorologists in Mexico have reported a drop in the average temperature over the past few months.

In years past, average temperatures for this time of year were in the upper 80s to 90 degrees. This year, the average high temperature was 85.

People in Mexico have enjoyed below-normal temperatures for the past three months. Scientists worry that this trend could carry over to winter, leaving a harsh winter in store for Mexico.

Eruption Rocks Mexico

By Boomen Hill

A volcano near the Pacific Ocean in Mexico exploded yesterday, sending tons of volcanic ash miles into the air.

The shock wave from the blast was felt as far away as Monterrey, Mexico, 200 miles away.

Mexican residents near the eruption were evacuated to shelters 30 miles from the volcano.

It is unknown when the residents will be allowed to return home. Many residents reported several feet of ash in the streets. Luckily, the volcano has only spouted ash.

Activity 41 - Weather Affects Earth

Instructional Materials
♦ student journals, and
♦ 3 large pieces of chart paper.

A. Have students form three teams. Give each team a large piece of chart paper.

B. Instruct each team to create a word web like the one below:

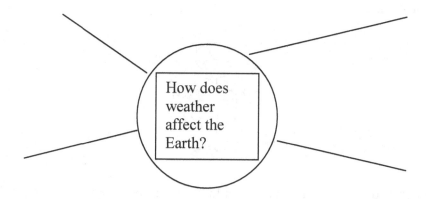

How does weather affect the Earth?

C. Have teams brainstorm large categories such as people and places. Then help them brainstorm subcategories under each large headings. Allow 20–30 minutes to brainstorm.

Closure
Invite teams to share their brainstorming with the class.

Extension
Challenge students to further research a topic they brainstormed, and encourage them to give a report to the class.

Assessment
Assess student-produced word webs.

Activity 42 – The Adventures of Weatherman

Instructional Materials
♦ a computer with Internet access.

Background Information
Meteorologists have a tough job, with millions of people depending on them to predict the next day's weather. But the weather is **unpredictable**. When a meteorologist forecasts a warm, sunny week and it turns out cold and rainy, some people blame the poor meteorologist.

A. Ask students to think about what it would be like to be a meteorologist. Ask whether students think people would be happy with their forecasts each day.

B. Share the Background Information.

C. Have students form pairs and challenge them to make a local meteorologist into a superhero, complete with a uniform and superpowers. Ask them: What would the superhero be able to do that no one else could? How would he or she help people?

D. Have students write stories or develop a comic strip about the meteorologist.

Closure
Invite students to share their stories.

Extensions
A. Invite the meteorologists featured by the students to talk about weather forecasting and to hear the stories about them.

B. Publish the stories on the Web site.

Assessment
Assess the meteorologist stories.

Activity 43 - Wonder Word Sort

Instructional Materials
♦ 6 copies of **Wonder Word Game Cards**, and
♦ envelopes.

Preparation
Cut each set of **Wonder Word Game Cards** apart and place them into separate envelopes.

A. Have students form six teams. Provide each team an envelope with **Wonder Word Game Cards** inside.

B. Inform teams that there are three categories of words inside each envelope. Explain that it is their job to sort the words into the categories. Category headings are in boldface type.

C. After 15–20 minute, invite teams to share how they categorized the words.

Closure
Distribute student journals and have students write to the following prompt:
How do you think all of the words from the game apply to Earth?

Extension
Challenge students to create word sort card games using weather and ocean words.

Assessment
Assess students' ability to correctly categorize the cards.

Wonder Word Game Cards

Ocean Geography	Ocean	Weather
guyot	wavelength	typhoon
rift valley	crest	tornado
continental slope	tsunami	eye wall
abyssal plains	ebb tide	jet stream
continental shelf	currents	typhoon

Activity 44 – Space Scramble

Instructional Materials
♦ chalkboard or overhead projector, and
♦ student journals.

Preparation
Copy **Scrambled Space** onto the chalkboard or a transparency before class. This will help you assess students' prior knowledge about Earth's atmosphere and space. Gather several books about Earth's atmosphere and space and place them in the research center.

A. Ask students to form pairs. Distribute journals and direct students' attention to the overhead or chalkboard. (See Preparation.)

B. Have students work as partners to complete the activity. Answers are listed below.
Part 1: Mercury, Venus, Earth, Mars, Jupiter, Saturn, Uranus, Neptune, Pluto
Part 2: The dark center is the terrasphere. The gray middle ring is the biosphere. The dotted outer layer is the atmosphere.
Part 3: Rockets have to go fast to escape Earth's gravity. Earth's atmosphere has five layers. Jupiter has 16 moons.

Closure
Invite students to share their answers.

Extensions
A. Invite students to write all they know about a topic concerning space or Earth's atmosphere. Have them share their writing with the class.

B. Challenge students to hypothesize how the Earth's atmosphere and its position in space are related to weather, oceans, and the inside of the Earth.

Assessment
Assess answers in student journals and the Closure activity.

Scrambled Space

Instructions

Part 1
Unscramble the following planet names. Then put them in order, from closest to the sun to farthest away.

sunev   usaurn   petenun

arms   heart   asrunt

lotup   ripejut   curryme

Part 2
Match the following diagram of Earth with the appropriate label.

atmosphere   terrasphere   biosphere

Part 3
Answer the following questions:
Why do rockets have to go so fast?
How many layers does Earth's atmosphere have?
Which planet has the most moons?

Activity 45 - Earth Is Unique

Instructional Materials
♦ computer with Internet access, and
♦ student journals.

Background Information
Of the nine planets in our solar system, only Earth supports life as we know it. Earth has an atmosphere made of nitrogen and oxygen, water, and is the perfect distance from the sun to support life. If Earth were any closer to the sun, it would be too hot to support life. Likewise, if Earth were any farther from the sun, it would be too cold to support life.

The **terrasphere** includes everything from the inside of the Earth to the surface. The **biosphere** is found at the surface of the Earth. This is where we live. The **atmosphere** extends around the biosphere and enables Earth to support life.

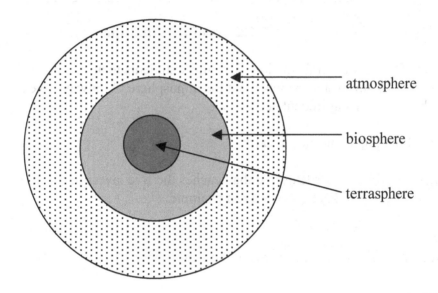

The atmosphere is divided into five layers. The bottom layer is called the **troposphere**. This is where we live. This is also where all of our weather occurs. The next layer is the **stratosphere**. Balloons and airplanes can fly at this level. The **mesosphere** is one of the coldest layers of the atmosphere, reaching -90°C. The **thermosphere** is the hottest layer of the atmosphere. Temperatures can reach 2000°C when heated by the sun's rays. The **exosphere** is the outer layer of the atmosphere. This layer touches space.

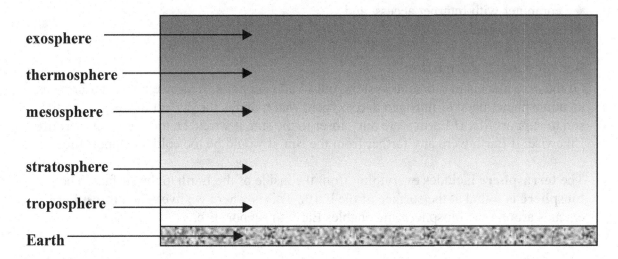

Layers of the Atmosphere

A. Share the Background Information, then allow students to access the following Web site. This site contains a short video about the atmosphere. As always, please preview the Web site before allowing student access.

http://www.brainpop.com/science/earth/

B. Challenge students to write a song that teaches the five layers of the atmosphere. Use the song on **There Are Five Layers** as an example.

Closure
Invite students to share their songs about the atmosphere.

Extensions
A. Ask permission for your students to go to another class to teach the songs they created about the atmosphere.

B. Publish the songs on the Web site, if you created one.

Assessment
Assess the songs students created.

There Are Five Layers

(sing to the tune of "Oh My Darlin'" or "Found a Peanut")

There are five layers, there are five layers
Five layers in the atmosphere.
There are five layers, there are five layers
Five layers in the atmosphere.

The stratosphere is the first layer of the atmosphere,
We live and breathe here, work and play dear,
It's a good place for you and me!

The troposphere is the second layer of the atmosphere,
Planes can fly here, balloons fly near dear,
Not an easy place for you and me!

The mesosphere is the third layer of the atmosphere,
Very cold here, not much air dear,
Not a good place for you and me!

The thermosphere is the fourth layer of the atmosphere,
Very hot here, burning hot dear,
A very bad place for you and me!

The exosphere is the last layer of the atmosphere,
Air is thin here, touches space dear,
Let's get a spaceship to go and see!

Activity 46 - Sunny Days

Instructional Materials
♦ 5 large pieces of paper, and
♦ student journals.

Background Information
Space begins about 75 miles above Earth. Earth is part of a **solar system**. A solar system is a group of planets, comets, asteroids, and other space objects that revolve around a star. We call the star in our solar system the **sun**. The sun is just one of the stars that make up our **galaxy**. The millions of galaxies make up the infinite area we call the **universe**. Some scientists believe there is no end to the universe.

Our sun is a middle-aged yellow star. The hottest part of the sun is its center. It takes light from the sun 8 minutes to reach Earth. Light travels at 186,000 miles per second, so the sun is millions of miles away.

The sun is the largest object in our solar system. Over one million planets the size of Earth would fit inside the sun. We depend on the **energy** from the sun to survive. Without the sun's heat and light, life on Earth would cease to exist. The extinction of the dinosaurs may be an example of this. Many scientists believe this mass extinction occurred after an asteroid slammed into Earth. The asteroid caused tons of dust to enter Earth's atmosphere. The dust blocked out much of the sun's light and heat energy. Soon, the plants began to die. Then the plant-eating dinosaurs died. Finally, the meat-eating dinosaurs died.

A. Have students form five teams. Give each team a large piece of paper.

B. Challenge teams to brainstorm all the ways we depend on the sun. Ask the following questions to get students thinking.
♦ What depends on the sun to survive?
♦ How do we use the sun's energy?

C. Allow students to brainstorm for 20 minutes, then invite teams to share their brainstorming with the class.

D. Share the Background Information. Allow students to return to their lists to record any new ideas they got from listening to others and the Background Information.

Closure

A. Have students answer the following question in their journals: How do you depend on the sun?

B. Invite students to share their journal responses.

Extensions

A. Allow students to use books and the Internet to do more research about the sun. The following search engine provides many Web sites about the sun. As always, be sure to preview any Web site before allowing student access.

www.yahooligans.com

B. Invite students to publish their research and add it to the Web site.

Assessment

Assess student journal entries from the Closure activity.

Activity 47 - Without the Sun...

Instructional Materials
- 5 large pieces of paper, and
- student journals.

A. Have students form five teams. Provide each team a large piece of paper.

B. Challenge students to brainstorm all the ways Earth would be affected if the sun suddenly didn't exist.

C. After several minutes, ask students to brainstorm how their lives would be impacted if the sun didn't exist.

D. Invite teams to share their lists.

E. Have teams choose five huge problems that would occur if we had no sun. Then ask them to develop solutions to each problem. Ask students to consider whether we have the technology on Earth to survive without the sun.

F. Invite teams to share their problems and solutions with the class.

G. Share **Sun Facts** with students.

Closure
A. Ask students to answer the following question in their journals: How would your life be affected if the sun suddenly didn't exist? Ask students to elaborate on their previous answers from step C.

B. Invite students to share their writing.

Extensions

A. Have students form pairs. Challenge students to write a story about people living without the sun. Possible titles could include A Day Without the Sun, The Month the Sun Went Away, or No sun, No Fun!

B. Have students develop setting, characters, and plot. Remind students to develop a story line with a beginning, middle, and end.

C. Invite students to share their stories.

D. Publish the stories and add them to the Web site.

Assessment

Assess student journal writing during the Closure activity.

Sun Facts

1. The sun is the center of our solar system.

2. The sun is a middle-aged star that burns bright yellow.

3. The diameter (distance across the sun) is 864,000 miles.

4. The temperature inside the sun is 15 million degrees.

5. Light from the sun takes 8 minutes to get to the Earth traveling at 186,000 miles per second.

6. The sun spins on its axis from left to right.

7. The sun is 4.6 billion years old.

8. The core, the equator of the sun, the top, and the bottom all spin at different speeds.

9. A planet the size of Earth could fit inside the sun more than one million times.

10. The sun's surface, called the photosphere, churns and boils like something in a cooking pot.

11. The sun is not fixed in space. It is constantly moving. It's up to the planets and the moons to keep up as it travels its course.

12. The light that comes from the sun is equal to 4 trillion light bulbs.

13. When the sun was born it was 20 times larger and 100 times brighter than it is today.

14. On Jupiter the sun appears only 1/5 the size of what we see here on Earth.

15. It takes the sun 26 days to spin around one time.

Activity 48 – Build a Solar System

Instructional Materials
- *The Magic School Bus Lost in the Solar System* book, by Joanna Cole,
- student journals, and
- papier-mâché materials:
  2 old newspapers,
  1 large bowl,
  10 round balloons,
  string,
  flour,
  tempera paint (red, blue, yellow, and white), and
  paintbrushes.

Preparation
Decide before class whether you will have students make a papier-mâché model solar system or have them draw and label a solar system on a large piece of chart paper.

A. Select several students to read aloud *The Magic School Bus Lost in the Solar System*. Be sure they read all the notes off to the side of the main text.

B. After reading, ask the following questions:
- What can you learn about at a planetarium?
- What makes day and night?
- Why can't spaceships just fly into space?
- Why do people weigh less on the moon than they do on Earth?
- What are solar flares?
- Which planet is red? Why is it red?
- What are the inner planets? What are the outer planets?
- Why do you think the ice and dust in Saturn's rings travel in a circle around Saturn?

C. Invite students to study the solar system mobile created by Ms. Frizzle's class at the back of the book.

D. Provide copies of **Papier-Mâché Planets** if students will be making a 3-dimensional solar system. Have students follow the instructions to create a classroom solar system. Students may use the information on the chart in the back of the book to create a large chart of the solar system on butcher paper.

Closure

Ask students to respond to the following prompt in their journals: Write about your favorite planet. Why is it your favorite? What makes your planet unique from all others? How does knowing about your favorite planet help you better understand the Earth?

Extensions

A. Have students publish their writing about the planets and add it to the Web site. Be sure to include digital pictures of the solar system model.

B. Invite students from other classes to take a tour of the solar system.

Assessment

Assess journal writing from the Closure activity.

Papier-Mâché Planets

Instructional Materials

- *The Magic School Bus Lost in the Solar System* book, by Joanna Cole, and
- papier-mâché materials:
  2 old newspapers,
  1 large bowl,
  10 round balloons,
  string,
  flour,
  water,
  glue,
  tempera paint (red, blue, yellow, white), and
  paintbrushes.

Instructions

1. Choose a partner, then select a planet to make for the 3-dimensional solar system in your classroom. One partner pair will need to make the sun.

2. Cover your work areas with newspaper. Tear the rest of the newspaper into one-inch strips and place them in a pile.

3. Each pair of students needs one balloon. Refer to the chart in the back of *The Magic School Bus Lost in the Solar System* to determine how large to inflate each balloon. The sun should be the largest balloon and Pluto should be the smallest. Inflate and tie your balloon.

4. In a large bowl, mix a paste of 1 cup of flour, 2 cups of water, and 1 handful of glue.

5. Dip strips of newspaper in the paste and squeeze the strips through your fingers to remove excess paste. Place the strips across the balloon. Cover the entire balloon with strips of newspaper.

6. Take your projects to the designated drying area. They'll need to dry for one to four days, depending on temperature, air circulation, and humidity.

7. While your project is drying, write a report about your planet or the sun to present to the class. Use books in your classroom to help you. Be sure to include the information from the chart at the back of the book.

8. When your project is dry, look at pictures to determine what color or colors to paint it. Here is a quick color-mixing chart to help you:

red + yellow = orange
blue + yellow = green
blue + red = purple
blue + red + yellow = brown

9. Hang your planet or sun from the ceiling with string. Have your teacher help you decide where your planet should hang.

Activity 49 - Many Moons

Instructional Materials
♦ *The Magic School Bus Lost in the Solar System* book, by Joanna Cole,
♦ student journals, and
♦ 1 copy of **Moon Math** per student.

Background Information
Two planets in our solar system do not have moons, Mercury and Venus. Earth has one moon and Mars has two. The chart at the back of *The Magic School Bus Lost in the Solar System* shows that Jupiter, Saturn, Uranus, and Neptune have many moons each. Pluto has only one moon.

The effect of the moon on Earth is great. We know that the gravity caused by the pull of the moon causes tides in the oceans. The gravity must be incredibly strong to move entire oceans on Earth. Moons are called **satellites**. Satellites are objects that **orbit** a planet.

The moon is the only place in our solar system besides Earth where man has been. On July 20, 1969, astronauts first set foot on the moon. Since then, astronauts have gone to the moon five times. Astronauts encountered a harsh climate on the moon. There was no air, and temperatures ranged from 250°F in the sun (that's hotter than boiling water) to -290°F in the dark. Fortunately, the astronauts had space suits to protect them from these extreme temperatures.

A. Distribute copies of **Moon Math** and allow students to work in pairs to complete the math problems.
Answers: 1. 0; 2. 32; 3. 40; 4. 0; 5. 18; 6. 2

B. Teach the order of the planets using a mnemonic device. Try this one:

My **V**ery **E**xcited **M**utt **J**umped **S**ixty **U**naware **N**apping **P**oodles

C. Challenge students to develop their own mnemonic sentences to remember the order of the planets.

Closure

A. Have students write in their journals about what they think life would be like on the moon.

B. Share the Background Information, then have students write to the following prompt in their journals: Write about how the moon affects the Earth. Consider Saturn with 18 moons. How do you think the moons affect Saturn? How would life be different on Earth if we had 18 moons? How would life on Earth be different if we had no moons?

Extensions

A. Have students research the moon to better determine what life would be like there. Challenge students to write a story about building a space station on the moon. Ask them to compare life on Earth to life in a space station on the moon.

B. If you created a Web site, have them publish their research about the moon to the site.

Assessment

Assess students writing in the Closure section.

Moon Math

Complete the following problems using the moon chart below.

Planet	Number of Moons
Mercury	0
Venus	0
Earth	1
Mars	2
Jupiter	16
Saturn	18
Uranus	15
Neptune	8
Pluto	1

1. Mercury x Saturn = _____

2. Jupiter x Mars = _____

3. Neptune + Jupiter + Uranus + Pluto = _____

4. Uranus x Jupiter x Venus = _____

5. Earth x Saturn = _____

6. Jupiter / Neptune =

Now create 5 Moon Math problems of your own.

Activity 50 - Planet Water

Instructional Materials
♦ student journals, and
♦ 1 copy of **The Way the World Works** for each student.

Background Information
During this activity, students will consider everything learned during Earth Central as they answer questions. Students will realize that all of the physical aspects of Earth and its place in the solar system work together to support life as we know it.

A. Distribute copies of **The Way the World Works**. Encourage students to answer each question as completely as possible.

B. Tell students that Earth Central is almost over. Encourage students to plan a party to show their families what they have learned.

C. Decide on a time to have the party and provide art materials for students to use to make invitations for their families.

D. Encourage students to brainstorm all of the projects they have completed during Earth Central. Have students display the projects so that parents can see what was learned.

E. Have students plan what refreshments (if any) they would like to have at the Earth Central party. Encourage students to share the responsibility of bringing food and drinks.

Closure
Have students write to the following prompt in their journals: Write about your favorite part of Earth Central. What was the most fascinating thing you learned?

Extension
Have students develop a game to be played at the party. The game should include questions that can be answered with knowledge gained from Earth Central. Here are some game ideas:
♦ create a Jeopardy!-style game,
♦ create a concentration game, or
♦ create a baseball game in which questions must be answered to move to the next base.

Assessment
Assess student journal entries and answers on **The Way the World Works**.

The Way the World Works

Instructions

Answer the following questions as completely as you can. Use all the information you have learned during Earth Central to help you. You may also draw pictures to help you answer the questions.

1. How does the inside of Earth affect the surface of the Earth (both land and oceans)?

2. How does the surface (both land and oceans) of the Earth affect the weather?

3. How can the inside of the Earth affect the weather?

4. How does the sun affect the Earth?

5. How does the moon affect the Earth?

Activity 51 - Earth Quiz 2

Instructional Materials
♦ 1 copy of **Hello, This Is Planet Earth** (from Activity 2) per student.

Preparation
Arrange the room to give the content assessment to students. You may choose to move desks around so students are not tempted to work together on the assessment.

A. Explain to students that you want to see what they have learned from Earth Central, then distribute copies of **Hello, This Is Planet Earth**. Provide as much time as needed to finish the assessment. Compare the pre- and post-assessment scores to determine what students have learned.

B. When everyone has finished the assessment, invite each student to share his or her favorite part of Earth Central.

C. Help students prepare the room for the Earth Central party.

D. Have students take their parents on a tour of everything they learned during Earth Central.

Earth Central
Vocabulary and Materials Checklist

*Order Forms Supplied for this resource.

Note: Paper and pencils should be on-hand each day, as should writing and illustration supplies, and may not be listed on the Checklist.

Activity	Vocabulary	Materials Needed
1	experiment hypothesis observation prediction theory	6 large sheets of chart paper, and a computer with Internet access.
2		1 copy of **Hello, This is Planet Earth** per student, and 20 sheets of notebook paper per student.
3	core crust inner core mantle molten outer core	old newspaper, (1) 12-inch round balloon per student, 4 cups of flour, glue, 4 large bowls, tempera paint (red, blue, yellow), string, and a computer with Internet access.
4	fortify	3 Nails for Breakfast kits from The Wild Goose Company*, 3 shallow plates or dishes, 3 spoons, a computer with Internet access, and **Optional:** small boxes of three other breakfast cereals that are fortified with iron.
5	composition Jules Verne	1 spoon per team, 1 ruler per team, stopwatch or watch with a second hand, computer with Internet access, and **Optional:** a calculator.
6	climatology continental drift meteorology Pangaea revolution supercontinent	Scientific Method posters (created in Activity 1), 3 copies of **Pangaea Jigsaw**, 3 copies of **World Map**, 3 copies of **News Flash!**, and a computer with Internet access.
7	legend myths	**Optional:** props for myth plays
8	fault	books about earthquakes

	friction magma tremors	a computer with Internet access, and student journals.
9	absorb architects engineers	materials to build structures, such as dominoes, playing cards, blocks, and toilet paper rolls; several markers; several text books; and materials to absorb the shock of student-generated earthquakes, such as foam rubber, wooden blocks, and cotton.
10	catastrophic epicenter magnitude seismograph seismologist Richter scale tremor	1 copy of **A Whole Lot of Shakin' Goin' On!** for each team, a computer with Internet access, and resource materials about earthquakes.
11		resources about earthquakes.
12		1 copy of **Geological Loop Game Cards**.
13	geophysicist geophysics prefix root word specializations suffix	several dictionaries.
14	central vent cone crater magma chamber sill volcano	books about volcanoes, and a computer with Internet access.
15	active dormant extinct lava Mauna Kea Roman Vulcan	copies of **World Map** from Activity 6, 1 piece of centimeter graph paper per two students.
16	island chain	*The Magic School Bus Blows Its Top* book, by Gail Herman; *The Magic School Bus Inside the Earth* book, by Joanna Cole; and a computer with Internet access.
17	ingredients	See Activity 17 for materials list.
18	mud flows	A computer with Internet access.

	tsunamis	books about volcanoes, and copies of **World Map** from Activity 6.
19	goddess Kamapuaa Pele	books about volcanoes.
20	insulated	copies of **The Volcano Olympians** for each team, and **Optional:** calculators.
21	diameter insulated slope viscous	1 bottle of thick chocolate syrup (refrigerated), 1 bottle of lite (runny) maple syrup (refrigerated), 1 cookie sheet, 1 empty wrapping paper roll, 1 clock, and a computer with Internet access.
22	deep-sea vents submersible	3 copies of **Discoveries;** *Fountains of Life The Story of Deep-Sea Vents* book, by Elizabeth Tayntnor Gowell; and A computer with Internet access.
23	landforms	books about various landforms such as mountains, the Grand Canyon, geysers, glaciers, caves, etc.; and a computer with Internet access.
24		1 copy of **Ring of Fire Game Cards**.
25		6 copies of **Sea Sort Game Cards**, and several books about the ocean.
26	Arctic Antarctic Atlantic Indian ocean Pacific	1 globe, 1 large world map, 1 package of sticky notes or stick dots, and books about oceans for the research area.
27	cohesive hemisphere meniscus properties surface tension	3 small bowls, 3 pennies, 3 straws, pepper, 3 needles, liquid soap, and 3 copies of **Tension Experiments**.
28	Marianas Trench obstacles pressure	(1) 2-liter bottle per team, 1 large baking dish per team, and a computer with Internet access.
29	density dissolving mass salinity	salt, 5 clear plastic cups, 2 large pitchers, very hot water, very cold water, and

		red, blue, and yellow food coloring.
30	abyssal plains continental shelf continental rise continental slope guyots mountain ridges rift valleys seamounts shoreline trenches	A computer with Internet access.
31	mural	*The Magic School Bus on the Ocean Floor* book, by Joanna Cole; 2 large sheets of butcher paper; and a computer with Internet access.
32	diagrams	copies (or transparency) of **Ocean Song**.
33	breaks crest trough wave wavelength	1 transparent glass baking dish, blue food coloring, computer with Internet access, and **Optional:** (1) 2-liter bottle with labels removed, 1 bottle of rubbing alcohol, and 1 bottle of baby oil.
34	astrological ebb tide flood tide gravitational high tide tide pools	1 wire hanger per student, 1 copy of **Tide Mobile, Tide 1, Tide 2**, and **Tide Mobile Patterns** for each student, and yarn.
35	currents equator polar regions prevailing winds	
36	Aristotle climate forecasting meteorology	several books about weather, storms, water cycle, etc.; 1 large sheet of butcher paper; 3 Wild Wacky Weather kits from The Wild Goose Company*; 1 hair dryer; 4 adult volunteers; 1 current newspaper; and **Optional:** 1 outdoor thermometer, and 1 rain gauge.
37	condensation evaporation molecules	◆ weather chart from Activity 36, ◆ weather instruments, ◆ metal cake or sheet pan,

	precipitation water vapor	◆ ice cubes, ◆ large glass jar, and ◆ computer with Internet access.
38	cyclones equator eye eye wall hurricanes squall lines tropical depression tropical storm typhoons	*The Magic School Bus Inside a Hurricane* book, by Joanna Cole; 1 bowl filled with water; 1 small piece of Styrofoam; 1 glass of water; 3 copies of **Hurricane in a Bowl**; 3 copies of **Hurricane Movie Magic**; 3 medium boxes, 6 paper towel rolls, and a computer with Internet access.
39	cell downdrafts rotate Tornado Alley tornadoes updrafts	3 copies of **Terribly Terrific Tongue Twisters**, 3 Wild Wacky Weather kits from the Wild Goose Company*, 6 plastic soda bottles (2-liter), food coloring, and a computer with Internet access.
40	jet stream	a computer with Internet access, and 3 copies of **In the News.**
41		3 large pieces of chart paper.
42	unpredictable	computer with Internet access.
43		6 copies of **Wonder Word Game Cards**, and 6 envelopes.
44		overhead projector.
45	atmosphere biosphere terrasphere	a computer with Internet access.
46	galaxy solar system sun universe	5 large pieces of paper.
47		5 large pieces of paper.
48	inner planets outer planets planetarium solar flares	*The Magic School Bus Lost in the Solar System* book, by Joanna Cole; 2 old newspapers; 1 large bowl; 10 round balloons; string; flour; tempera paint (red, blue, yellow, and white); and paintbrushes.
49	orbit satellites	*The Magic School Bus Lost in the Solar System* book, by Joanna Cole.

		1 copy of **Moon Math** per student.
50		1 copy of **The Way the World Works** per student.
51		1 copy of **Hello, This is Planet Earth** per student.

Earth Central
TEKS Checklist

Activity	TEKS: Reading Language Arts	TEKS: Mathematics	TEKS: Social Studies	TEKS: Science
1	Connect his/her own experiences, information, insights, and ideas with those of others through speaking and listening Select, organize, or produce visuals to complement and extend meanings Use multiple sources, including electronic texts, experts, and print resources, to locate information relevant to research questions Study word meanings systematically such as across curricular content areas and through current events Write to entertain such as to compose humorous poems or short stories		Communicate in written, oral, and visual forms Write to inform such as to explain, describe, report, and narrate	Analyze and interpret information to construct reasonable explanations from direct and indirect evidence Plan and implement descriptive investigations including asking well-defined questions, formulating testable hypotheses, and selecting and using equipment and technology Analyze, review, and critique scientific explanations, including hypotheses and theories, as to their strengths and weaknesses using scientific evidence and information

Activity	TEKS: Reading Language Arts	TEKS: Mathematics	TEKS: Social Studies	TEKS: Science
2	Answer different types and levels of questions such as open-ended, literal, and interpretive as well as test-like questions such as multiple choice, true-false, and short answer			

Activity	TEKS: Reading Language Arts	TEKS: Mathematics	TEKS: Social Studies	TEKS: Science
3	Study word meanings systematically such as across curricular content areas and through current events Use multiple sources, including electronic texts, experts, and print resources, to locate information relevant to research questions Write to express, discover, record, develop, reflect on ideas, and to problem solve Select, organize, or produce visuals to complement and extend meanings		Analyze information by sequencing, categorizing, identifying cause-and-effect relationships, comparing, contrasting, finding the main idea, summarizing, making generalizations and predictions, and drawing inferences and conclusions Organize and interpret information in outlines, reports, databases, and visuals including graphs, charts, timelines, and maps	Represent the natural world using models and identify their limitations Predict and draw conclusions about what happens when part of a system is removed
4	Study word meanings systematically such as across curricular content areas and through current events Write to express, discover,	Estimate and measure capacity using standard units including milliliters, liters, cups, pints, quarts, and gallons Identify the mathematics in	Analyze information by sequencing, categorizing, identifying cause-and-effect relationships, comparing, contrasting, finding the main idea, summarizing, making	Conduct tests, compare data, and draw conclusions about physical properties of matter including states of matter, conduction, density, and buoyancy

Activity	TEKS: Reading Language Arts	TEKS: Mathematics	TEKS: Social Studies	TEKS: Science
	record, develop, reflect on ideas, and to problem solve Use multiple sources, including electronic texts, experts, and print resources, to locate information relevant to research questions	everyday situations Use tools such as real objects, manipulatives, and technology to solve problems	generalizations and predictions, and drawing inferences and conclusions	Collect and analyze information using tools including calculators, safety goggles, microscopes, cameras, sound recorders, computers, hand lenses, meter sticks, timing devices, balances, and compasses Demonstrate that repeated investigations may increase the reliability of the results Collect information by observing and measuring Analyze and interpret information to construct reasonable explanations from direct and indirect evidence Communicate valid conclusions Analyze, review, and critique scientific explanations, including hypotheses and theories, as to their strengths and weaknesses using scientific evidence and information

Activity	TEKS: Reading Language Arts	TEKS: Mathematics	TEKS: Social Studies	TEKS: Science
5	Study word meanings systematically such as across curricular content areas and through current events Write to express, discover, record, develop, reflect on ideas, and to problem solve	Explain and record observations using objects, words, pictures, numbers, and technology Identify the mathematics in everyday situations Select or develop an appropriate problem-solving strategy, including drawing a picture, looking for a pattern, systematic guessing and checking, acting it out, making a table, working a simpler problem, or working backwards to solve a problem Use tools such as real objects, manipulatives, and technology to solve problems Use lists, tables, charts, and diagrams to find patterns and make generalizations	Communicate in written, oral, and visual forms Write to inform such as to explain, describe, report, and narrate Create written and visual material such as journal entries, reports, graphic organizers, outlines, and bibliographies Organize and interpret information in outlines, reports, databases, and visuals including graphs, charts, timelines, and maps	Conduct tests, compare data, and draw conclusions about physical properties of matter including states of matter, conduction, density, and buoyancy Collect and analyze information using tools including calculators, safety goggles, microscopes, cameras, sound recorders, computers, hand lenses, meter sticks, timing devices, balances, and compasses Collect information by observing and measuring Analyze and interpret information to construct reasonable explanations from direct and indirect evidence
6	Write to express, discover, record, develop, reflect on ideas, and to problem solve Use multiple sources, including electronic texts, experts, and print resources, to locate and organize information Interpret important events and	Identify the mathematics in everyday situations Use addition and subtraction to solve problems Select or develop an appropriate problem-solving strategy	Communicate in written, oral, and visual forms Use problem-solving and decision-making skills Apply critical-thinking skills to organize and use information acquired from a variety of sources Identify different points of view	Plan and implement descriptive and simple experimental investigations including asking well-defined questions, formulating testable hypotheses, and selecting and using equipment and technology Collect information by observing and measuring

157

© Prufrock Press Inc.

Activity	TEKS: Reading Language Arts	TEKS: Mathematics	TEKS: Social Studies	TEKS: Science
	ideas gathered from maps, charts, graphics, video segments, or technology presentations Draw conclusions from information gathered from multiple sources Frame questions to direct research		about an issue or topic Offer observations, make connections, react, speculate, interpret, and raise questions in response to texts Create written and visual material such as journal entries, reports, graphic organizers, outlines, and bibliographies Organize and interpret information in outlines, reports, databases, and visuals including graphs, charts, timelines, and maps	Communicate valid conclusions Analyze, review, and critique scientific explanations, including hypotheses and theories, as to their strengths and weaknesses using scientific evidence and information
7	Study word meanings systematically such as across curricular content areas and through current events Write to express, discover, record, develop, reflect on ideas, and to problem solve Write to entertain such as to compose humorous poems or short stories Understand literary forms by recognizing and distinguishing among such types of text as stories, poems, myths, fables, tall tales, limericks, plays, biographies, and		Offer observations, make connections, react, speculate, interpret, and raise questions in response to texts Communicate in written, oral, and visual forms Create written and visual material such as journal entries, reports, graphic organizers, outlines, and bibliographies	

Activity	TEKS: Reading Language Arts	TEKS: Mathematics	TEKS: Social Studies	TEKS: Science
	autobiographies			
8	Study word meanings systematically such as across curricular content areas and through current events Use multiple sources, including electronic texts, experts, and print resources, to locate and organize information	Identify the mathematics in everyday situations	Use appropriate mathematical skills to interpret social studies information such as maps and graphs Create written and visual material such as journal entries, reports, graphic organizers, outlines, and bibliographies Organize and interpret information in outlines, reports, databases, and visuals including graphs, charts, timelines, and maps	Plan and implement descriptive and simple experimental investigations including asking well-defined questions, formulating testable hypotheses, and selecting and using equipment and technology Collect information by observing and measuring Communicate valid conclusions Analyze and interpret information to construct reasonable explanations from direct and indirect evidence Represent the natural world using models and identify their limitations Predict and draw conclusions about what happens when part of a system is removed Analyze, review, and critique scientific explanations, including hypotheses and theories, as to their strengths and weaknesses using scientific evidence and information
9	Study word meanings systematically such as across	Identify the mathematics in everyday situations	Communicate in written, oral, and visual forms	Plan and implement descriptive and simple experimental

Activity	TEKS: Reading Language Arts	TEKS: Mathematics	TEKS: Social Studies	TEKS: Science
	curricular content areas and through current events Draw conclusions from information gathered from multiple sources Write to express, discover, record, develop, reflect on ideas, and to problem solve		Create written and visual material such as journal entries, reports, graphic organizers, outlines, and bibliographies	investigations including asking well-defined questions, formulating testable hypotheses, and selecting and using equipment and technology Collect information by observing and measuring Analyze and interpret information to construct reasonable explanations from direct and indirect evidence Represent the natural world using models and identify their limitations Predict and draw conclusions about what happens when part of a system is removed Analyze, review, and critique scientific explanations, including hypotheses and theories, as to their strengths and weaknesses using scientific evidence and information
10	Study word meanings systematically such as across curricular content areas and through current events Write to express, discover, record, develop, reflect on		Communicate in written, oral, and visual forms Express ideas orally based on research and experiences Create written and visual material	

© Prufrock Press Inc.

Activity	TEKS: Reading Language Arts	TEKS: Mathematics	TEKS: Social Studies	TEKS: Science
	ideas, and to problem solve		such as journal entries, reports, graphic organizers, outlines, and bibliographies	
	Use multiple sources, including electronic texts, experts, and print resources, to locate and organize information			
	Summarize and organize ideas gained from multiple sources in useful ways such as outlines, conceptual maps, learning logs, and timelines			
	Evaluate his/her own research and raise new questions for further investigation			
	Present information in various forms using available technology			
11	Write to entertain such as to compose humorous poems or short stories			
	Evaluate how well his/her own writing achieves its purposes			

Activity	TEKS: Reading Language Arts	TEKS: Mathematics	TEKS: Social Studies	TEKS: Science
12	Analyze published examples as models for writing Draw inferences such as conclusions or generalizations and support them with text evidence and experience	Identify the mathematics in everyday situations		
13	Study word meanings systematically such as across curricular content areas and through current events Use structural analysis to identify root words with prefixes such as *dis-, non-, in-;* and suffixes such as *—ness, -tion, -able* Locate meanings, pronunciations, and derivations of unfamiliar words using dictionaries, glossaries, and other sources Write to entertain such as to compose humorous poems or short stories			

Activity	TEKS: Reading Language Arts	TEKS: Mathematics	TEKS: Social Studies	TEKS: Science
14	Study word meanings systematically such as across curricular content areas and through current events		Communicate in written, oral, and visual forms	Analyze and interpret information to construct reasonable explanations from direct and indirect evidence
	Use multiple sources, including electronic texts, experts, and print resources, to locate and organize information		Express ideas orally based on research and experiences	Represent the natural world using models and identify their limitations
	Write to express, discover, record, develop, reflect on ideas, and to problem solve		Create written and visual material such as journal entries, reports, graphic organizers, outlines, and bibliographies	
	Evaluate his/her own research and raise new questions for further investigation			
	Present information in various forms using available technology			
	Use available technology to support aspects of creating, revising, editing, and publishing texts			

163

Activity	TEKS: Reading Language Arts	TEKS: Mathematics	TEKS: Social Studies	TEKS: Science
15	Study word meanings systematically such as across curricular content areas and through current events	Select or develop an appropriate problem-solving strategy, including drawing a picture, looking for a pattern, systematic guessing and checking, acting it out, making a table, working a simpler problem, or working backwards to solve a problem	Create written and visual material such as journal entries, reports, graphic organizers, outlines, and bibliographies	Analyze and interpret information to construct reasonable explanations from direct and indirect evidence
	Locate meanings, pronunciations, and derivations of unfamiliar words using dictionaries, glossaries, and other sources	Use tools such as real objects, manipulatives, and technology to solve problems	Communicate in written, oral, and visual forms	Communicate valid conclusions
	Select, organize, or produce visuals to complement and extend meanings	Use lists, tables, charts, and diagrams to find patterns and make generalizations	Organize and interpret information in outlines, reports, databases, and visuals including graphs, charts, timelines, and maps	Analyze, review, and critique scientific explanations, including hypotheses and theories, as to their strengths and weaknesses using scientific evidence and information
	Draw conclusions from information gathered from multiple sources			
	Write to express, discover, record, develop, reflect on ideas, and to problem solve			
	Use multiple sources, including electronic texts, experts, and print resources, to locate and organize information			

Activity	TEKS: Reading Language Arts	TEKS: Mathematics	TEKS: Social Studies	TEKS: Science
16	Recognize that authors organize information in specific ways		Create written and visual material such as journal entries, reports, graphic organizers, outlines, and bibliographies	Analyze and interpret information to construct reasonable explanations from direct and indirect evidence
	Identify the purposes of different types of texts such as to inform, influence, express, or entertain		Communicate in written, oral, and visual forms	
	Draw inferences such as conclusions or generalizations and support them with text evidence and experience			
	Find similarities and differences across texts such as in treatment, scope, or organization			
	Answer different types and levels of questions such as open-ended, literal, and interpretive as well as test-like questions such as multiple choice, true-false, and short answer			

Activity	TEKS: Reading Language Arts	TEKS: Mathematics	TEKS: Social Studies	TEKS: Science
17	Read for varied purposes such as to be informed, to be entertained, to appreciate the writer's craft, and to discover models for his/her own writing	Estimate and measure capacity using standard units including milliliters, liters, cups, pints, quarts, and gallons	Create written and visual material such as journal entries, reports, graphic organizers, outlines, and bibliographies	Demonstrate safe practices during field and laboratory investigations
	Use available technology to support aspects of creating, revising, editing, and publishing texts	Identify the mathematics in everyday situations	Communicate in written, oral, and visual forms	
	Write to express, discover, record, develop, reflect on ideas, and to problem solve	Use tools such as real objects, manipulatives, and technology to solve problems		
18	Read for varied purposes such as to be informed, to be entertained, to appreciate the writer's craft, and to discover models for his/her own writing	Identify the mathematics in everyday situations	Organize and interpret information in outlines, reports, databases, and visuals including graphs, charts, timelines, and maps	Analyze and interpret information to construct reasonable explanations from direct and indirect evidence
	Use available technology to support aspects of creating, revising, editing, and publishing texts			Represent the natural world using models and identify their limitations
	Use multiple sources, including electronic texts, experts, and print resources, to locate and organize information			Predict and draw conclusions about what happens when part of a system is removed
	Evaluate his/her own research and raise new questions for further investigation			

166

Activity	TEKS: Reading Language Arts	TEKS: Mathematics	TEKS: Social Studies	TEKS: Science
	Present information in various forms using available technology			
19	Write to entertain such as to compose humorous poems or short stories Understand literary forms by recognizing and distinguishing among such types of text as stories, poems, myths, fables, tall tales, limericks, plays, biographies, and autobiographies Use available technology to support aspects of creating, revising, editing, and publishing texts Present information in various forms using available technology		Communicate in written, oral, and visual forms	

167

Activity	TEKS: Reading Language Arts	TEKS: Mathematics	TEKS: Social Studies	TEKS: Science
20	Draw conclusions from information gathered from multiple sources

Support responses by referring to relevant aspects of text and his/her own experiences

Establish and adjust purposes for reading such as reading to find out, to understand, to interpret, to enjoy, and to solve problems | Use addition and subtraction to solve problems involving whole numbers

Use multiplication to solve problems involving two-digit numbers

Estimate a product or quotient beyond basic facts

Select or develop an appropriate problem-solving strategy, including drawing a picture, looking for a pattern, systematic guessing and checking, acting it out, making a table, working a simpler problem, or working backwards to solve a problem | Communicate in written, oral, and visual forms | |
| 21 | Use available technology to support aspects of creating, revising, editing, and publishing texts

Write to express, discover, record, develop, reflect on ideas, and to problem solve

Study word meanings systematically such as across curricular content areas and through current events

Draw conclusions from | Identify the mathematics in everyday situations

Use tools such as real objects, manipulatives, and technology to solve problems | Analyze, review, and critique scientific explanations, including hypotheses and theories, as to their strengths and weaknesses using scientific evidence and information | Analyze and interpret information to construct reasonable explanations from direct and indirect evidence

Represent the natural world using models and identify their limitations

Predict and draw conclusions about what happens when part of a system is removed

Plan and implement descriptive and simple experimental |

Activity	TEKS: Reading Language Arts	TEKS: Mathematics	TEKS: Social Studies	TEKS: Science
	information gathered from multiple sources Use multiple sources, including electronic texts, experts, and print resources, to locate and organize information			investigations including asking well-defined questions, formulating testable hypotheses, and selecting and using equipment and technology Collect information by observing and measuring
22	Use his/her knowledge and experience to comprehend Draw inferences such as conclusions or generalizations and support them with text evidence and experience Connect his/her own experiences, information, insights, and ideas with those of others through speaking and listening Use multiple sources, including electronic texts, experts, and print resources, to locate and organize information		Communicate in written, oral, and visual forms	Identify and describe the roles of some organisms in living systems such as plants in a schoolyard, and parts in nonliving systems such as a light bulb in a circuit Plan and implement descriptive and simple experimental investigations including asking well-defined questions, formulating testable hypotheses, and selecting and using equipment and technology Collect information by observing and measuring Compare adaptive characteristics of various species Analyze, review, and critique scientific explanations, including hypotheses and theories, as to their strengths and weaknesses using scientific evidence and information

169

Activity	TEKS: Reading Language Arts	TEKS: Mathematics	TEKS: Social Studies	TEKS: Science
	Use multiple sources, including electronic texts, experts, and print resources, to locate and organize information Connect his/her own experiences, information, insights, and ideas with those of others through speaking and listening		Communicate in written, oral, and visual forms	Identify and observe effects of events that require time for changes to be noticeable including growth, erosion, dissolving, weathering, and flow Analyze, review, and critique scientific explanations, including hypotheses and theories, as to their strengths and weaknesses using scientific evidence and information
23	Write to express, discover, record, develop, reflect on ideas, and to problem solve Use available technology to support aspects of creating, revising, editing, and publishing texts Present information in various forms using available technology			
24	Answer different types and levels of questions such as open-ended, literal, and interpretive as well as test-like questions such as multiple choice, true-false, and short answer			
25	Study word meanings systematically such as across curricular content areas and			Analyze and interpret information to construct reasonable explanations from direct and

Activity	TEKS: Reading Language Arts	TEKS: Mathematics	TEKS: Social Studies	TEKS: Science
	through current events			indirect evidence
	Use his/her own knowledge to comprehend			Communicate valid conclusions
26	Summarize and organize information from multiple sources of information by taking notes, outlining ideas, or making charts	Use lists, tables, charts, and diagrams to find patterns and make generalizations	Communicate in written, oral, and visual forms	Summarize the affects of the oceans on land
	Write to express, discover, record, develop, reflect on ideas, and to problem solve	Interpret bar graphs	Organize and interpret information in outlines, reports, databases, and visuals including graphs, charts, timelines, and maps	Analyze, review, and critique scientific explanations, including hypotheses and theories, as to their strengths and weaknesses using scientific evidence and information
		Justify why an answer is reasonable and explain the solution process		Plan and implement descriptive and simple experimental investigations including asking well-defined questions, formulating testable hypotheses, and selecting and using equipment and technology
				Collect information by observing and measuring
27	Write to express, discover, record, develop, reflect on ideas, and to problem solve	Identify the mathematics in everyday situations		Plan and implement descriptive and simple experimental investigations including asking well-defined questions, formulating testable hypotheses, and selecting and using equipment and technology
	Study word meanings systematically such as across curricular content areas and through current events			Collect information by observing and measuring
	Draw conclusions from information gathered from			

171

Activity	TEKS: Reading Language Arts	TEKS: Mathematics	TEKS: Social Studies	TEKS: Science
	multiple sources Use multiple sources, including electronic texts, experts, and print resources, to locate and organize information			Communicate valid conclusions
28	Use his/her knowledge and experience to comprehend Draw inferences such as conclusions or generalizations and support them with text evidence and experience Connect his/her own experiences, information, insights, and ideas with those of others through speaking and listening Use multiple sources, including electronic texts, experts, and print resources, to locate and organize information	Estimate and measure capacity using standard units including milliliters, liters, cups, pints, quarts, and gallons Identify the mathematics in everyday situations Use tools such as real objects, manipulatives, and technology to solve problems	Express ideas orally based on research and experiences Create written and visual material such as journal entries, reports, graphic organizers, outlines, and bibliographies	Plan and implement descriptive and simple experimental investigations including asking well-defined questions, formulating testable hypotheses, and selecting and using equipment and technology Collect information by observing and measuring Communicate valid conclusions
29	Draw inferences such as conclusions or generalizations and support them with text evidence and experience Connect his/her own experiences, information, insights, and ideas with those		Create written and visual material such as journal entries, reports, graphic organizers, outlines, and bibliographies	Plan and implement descriptive and simple experimental investigations including asking well-defined questions, formulating testable hypotheses, and selecting and using equipment and technology

172

Activity	TEKS: Reading Language Arts	TEKS: Mathematics	TEKS: Social Studies	TEKS: Science
	of others through speaking and listening			Collect information by observing and measuring Communicate valid conclusions Observe and record changes in the states of matter caused by the addition or reduction of heat Summarize the affects of oceans on land Make wise choices in the use and conservation of resources and the disposal or recycling of materials
30	Study word meanings systematically such as across curricular content areas and through current events Connect, compare, and contrast ideas, themes, and issues across texts Write to entertain such as to compose humorous poems or short stories		Create written and visual material such as journal entries, reports, graphic organizers, outlines, and bibliographies	
31	Use his/her own knowledge and experience to comprehend Distinguish fact and opinion in various texts		Create written and visual material such as journal entries, reports, graphic organizers, outlines, and bibliographies	Summarize the affects of the oceans on land Represent the natural world using models and identify their limitations

Activity	TEKS: Reading Language Arts	TEKS: Mathematics	TEKS: Social Studies	TEKS: Science
32	Write to entertain such as to compose humorous poems or short stories Paraphrase and summarize text to recall, inform, and organize ideas Present information in various forms using available technology			
33	Study word meanings systematically such as across curricular content areas and through current events Draw inferences such as conclusions or generalizations and support them with text evidence and experience Use multiple sources, including electronic texts, experts, and print resources, to locate and organize information Use available technology to support aspects of creating, revising, editing, and publishing texts	Identify the mathematics in everyday situations	Create written and visual material such as journal entries, reports, graphic organizers, outlines, and bibliographies	Plan and implement descriptive and simple experimental investigations including asking well-defined questions, formulating testable hypotheses, and selecting and using equipment and technology Collect information by observing and measuring Communicate valid conclusions
34	Study word meanings systematically such as across		Create written and visual material such as journal entries, reports,	Summarize the affects of the oceans on land

Activity	TEKS: Reading Language Arts	TEKS: Mathematics	TEKS: Social Studies	TEKS: Science
	curricular content areas and through current events Present information in various forms using available technology Present dramatic interpretations of experiences, stories, poems, or plays to communicate		graphic organizers, outlines, and bibliographies	Represent the natural world using models and identify their limitations
35	Study word meanings systematically such as across curricular content areas and through current events Present dramatic interpretations of experiences, stories, poems, or plays to communicate Draw inferences such as conclusions or generalizations and support them with text evidence and experience			Analyze, review, and critique scientific explanations, including hypotheses and theories, as to their strengths and weaknesses using scientific evidence and information Predict and draw conclusions about what happens when part of a system is removed
36	Study word meanings systematically such as across curricular content areas and through current events Write to express, discover, record, develop, reflect on	Identify the mathematics in everyday situations Explain and record observations using objects, words, pictures, numbers, and technology	Create written and visual material such as journal entries, reports, graphic organizers, outlines, and bibliographies	Collect and analyze information using tools including calculators, microscopes, cameras, sound recorders, computers, hand lenses, rulers, thermometers, compasses, balances, hot plates, meter sticks, timing devices, magnets, collecting

175

Activity	TEKS: Reading Language Arts	TEKS: Mathematics	TEKS: Social Studies	TEKS: Science
	ideas, and to problem solve

Use available technology to support aspects of creating, revising, editing, and publishing texts | | | nets, and safety goggles |
| 37 | Study word meanings systematically such as across curricular content areas and through current events

Write to entertain such as to compose humorous poems or short stories | Identify the mathematics in everyday situations

Use tools such as real objects, manipulatives, and technology to solve problems

Use division to solve problems involving two-digit divisors | Create written and visual material such as journal entries, reports, graphic organizers, outlines, and bibliographies | Identify the Sun as the major source of energy for the Earth and understand its role in the growth of plants, in the creation or winds, and in the water cycle

Identify patterns of change such as in weather, metamorphosis, and objects in the sky

Analyze, review, and critique scientific explanations, including hypotheses and theories, as to their strengths and weaknesses using scientific evidence and information

Predict and draw conclusions about what happens when part of a system is removed

Plan and implement descriptive and simple experimental investigations including asking well-defined questions, formulating testable hypotheses, and selecting and using equipment and technology |

Activity	TEKS: Reading Language Arts	TEKS: Mathematics	TEKS: Social Studies	TEKS: Science
				Collect information by observing and measuring
				Communicate valid conclusions
38	Study word meanings systematically such as across curricular content areas and through current events		Create written and visual material such as journal entries, reports, graphic organizers, outlines, and bibliographies	Identify patterns of change such as in weather, metamorphosis, and objects in the sky
	Use multiple sources, including electronic texts, experts, and print resources, to locate and organize information			Analyze, review, and critique scientific explanations, including hypotheses and theories, as to their strengths and weaknesses using scientific evidence and information
	Determine a text's main (or major) ideas and how those ideas are supported with details			Predict and draw conclusions about what happens when part of a system is removed
	Draw inferences such as conclusions or generalizations and support them with text evidence and experience			Plan and implement descriptive and simple experimental investigations including asking well-defined questions, formulating testable hypotheses, and selecting and using equipment and technology
	Use available technology to support aspects of creating, revising, editing, and publishing texts			Collect information by observing and measuring
				Communicate valid conclusions
39	Connect his/her own experiences, information, insights, and ideas with those of others through speaking and		Communicate in written, oral, and visual forms	Evaluate the impact of research on scientific thought, society, and the environment
			Predict how future scientific	

Activity	TEKS: Reading Language Arts	TEKS: Mathematics	TEKS: Social Studies	TEKS: Science
	listening Offer observations, make connections, react, speculate, interpret, and raise questions in response to texts Use multiple sources, including electronic texts, experts, and print resources, to locate and organize information Write to entertain such as to compose humorous poems or short stories Select, organize, or produce visuals to complement and extend meanings		discoveries and technological innovations might affect life in Texas	Represent the natural world using models and identify their limitations
40	Study word meanings systematically such as across curricular content areas and through current events Connect his/her own experiences, information, insights, and ideas with those of others through speaking and listening Offer observations, make connections, react, speculate,		Express ideas orally based on research and experiences	Analyze, review, and critique scientific explanations, including hypotheses and theories, as to their strengths and weaknesses using scientific evidence and information

Activity	TEKS: Reading Language Arts	TEKS: Mathematics	TEKS: Social Studies	TEKS: Science
	interpret, and raise questions in response to texts Use multiple sources, including electronic texts, experts, and print resources, to locate and organize information			
41	Offer observations, make connections, react, speculate, interpret, and raise questions in response to texts Draw inferences such as conclusions or generalizations and support them with text evidence and experience			
42	Write to entertain such as to compose humorous poems or short stories		Create written and visual material such as journal entries, reports, graphic organizers, outlines, and bibliographies	
43	Study word meanings systematically such as across curricular content areas and through current events Use his/her own knowledge to comprehend			Analyze and interpret information to construct reasonable explanations from direct and indirect evidence Communicate valid conclusions
44	Answer different types and levels of questions such as open-ended, literal, and interpretive as well as test-like questions such as multiple choice, true-false, and short			

Activity	TEKS: Reading Language Arts	TEKS: Mathematics	TEKS: Social Studies	TEKS: Science
	answer			
	Draw inferences such as conclusions or generalizations and support them with text evidence and experience			
	Study word meanings systematically such as across curricular content areas and through current events		Create written and visual material such as journal entries, reports, graphic organizers, outlines, and bibliographies	Identify patterns of change such as in weather, metamorphosis, and objects in the sky
45	Use multiple sources, including electronic texts, experts, and print resources, to locate and organize information			
	Write to entertain such as to compose humorous poems or short stories			
	Present dramatic interpretations of experiences, stories, poems, or plays to communicate			
	Use available technology to support aspects of creating, revising, editing, and publishing texts			
46	Study word meanings systematically such as across curricular content areas and		Create written and visual material such as journal entries, reports, graphic organizers, outlines, and	Identify the Sun as the major source of energy for the Earth and understand its role in the growth of

Activity	TEKS: Reading Language Arts	TEKS: Mathematics	TEKS: Social Studies	TEKS: Science
	through current events		bibliographies	plants, in the creation or winds, and in the water cycle
	Use available technology to support aspects of creating, revising, editing, and publishing texts			
	Use multiple sources, including electronic texts, experts, and print resources, to locate and organize information			
47	Use multiple sources, including electronic texts, experts, and print resources, to locate and organize information		Create written and visual material such as journal entries, reports, graphic organizers, outlines, and bibliographies	Identify the Sun as the major source of energy for the Earth and understand its role in the growth of plants, in the creation or winds, and in the water cycle
	Draw inferences such as conclusions or generalizations and support them with text evidence and experience			Predict and draw conclusions about what happens when part of a system is removed
	Write to entertain such as to compose humorous poems or short stories			
	Use available technology to support aspects of creating, revising, editing, and publishing texts			
48	Produce research projects and reports in effective formats using visuals to support	Identify the mathematics in everyday situations	Create written and visual material such as journal entries, reports, graphic organizers, outlines, and	Identify patterns of change such as in weather, metamorphosis, and objects in the sky

Activity	TEKS: Reading Language Arts	TEKS: Mathematics	TEKS: Social Studies	TEKS: Science
	meaning, as appropriate Draw inferences such as conclusions or generalizations and support them with text evidence and experience Develop vocabulary by listening to selections read aloud	Explain and record observations using objects, words, pictures, numbers, and technology	bibliographies	
49	Draw inferences such as conclusions or generalizations and support them with text evidence and experience Offer observations, make connections, react, speculate, interpret, and raise questions in response to texts Write to express, discover, record, develop, reflect on ideas, and to problem solve	Use multiplication to solve problems involving two-digit numbers Use division to solve problems involving one-digit divisors Select of develop an appropriate problem-solving strategy, including drawing a picture, looking for a pattern, systematic guessing and checking, acting it out, making a table, working a simpler problem, or working backwards to solve a problem	Create written and visual material such as journal entries, reports, graphic organizers, outlines, and bibliographies	
50	Draw inferences such as conclusions or generalizations and support them with text evidence and experience Answer different types and levels of questions such as open-ended, literal, and interpretive as well as test-like		Create written and visual material such as journal entries, reports, graphic organizers, outlines, and bibliographies	Analyze and interpret information to construct reasonable explanations from direct and indirect evidence Communicate valid conclusions

Activity	TEKS: Reading Language Arts	TEKS: Mathematics	TEKS: Social Studies	TEKS: Science
	questions such as multiple choice, true-false, and short answer			
51	Answer different types and levels of questions such as open-ended, literal, and interpretive as well as test-like questions such as multiple choice, true-false, and short answer			

Printed in the United States
by Baker & Taylor Publisher Services